ISBN 978-0-243-08797-6
PIBN 10774730

1 MONTH OF
FREE
READING

at

www.ForgottenBooks.com

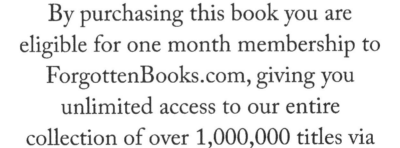

By purchasing this book you are eligible for one month membership to ForgottenBooks.com, giving you unlimited access to our entire collection of over 1,000,000 titles via our web site and mobile apps.

To claim your free month visit:

www.forgottenbooks.com/free774730

English
Français
Deutsche
Italiano
Español
Português

www.forgottenbooks.com

Mythology Photography **Fiction**
Fishing Christianity **Art** Cooking
Essays Buddhism Freemasonry
Medicine **Biology** Music **Ancient
Egypt** Evolution Carpentry Physics
Dance Geology **Mathematics** Fitness
Shakespeare **Folklore** Yoga Marketing
Confidence Immortality Biographies
Poetry **Psychology** Witchcraft
Electronics Chemistry History **Law**
Accounting **Philosophy** Anthropology
Alchemy Drama Quantum Mechanics
Atheism Sexual Health **Ancient History**
Entrepreneurship Languages Sport
Paleontology Needlework Islam
Metaphysics Investment Archaeology
Parenting Statistics Criminology
Motivational

PRACTICAL BAIT CASTING

BY

LARRY ST. JOHN

Illustrated with Photographs

Number 57

NEW YORK

THE MACMILLAN COMPANY

1918

Copyright, 1918, by

THE MACMILLAN COMPANY

———

THE FIRST CAST

This little book is not intended to be another contribution to that class of delightful reading known as "Angling Literature," but is an attempt to collect some of the traditions of the Craft, in more or less text book form, for the benefit of the beginner and the inexpert.

We hope the "old hand" will be sparing of his criticism—that he will keep in mind the fact that this is the first book on Practical Bait Casting; that we had no models to work on; that we are "blazing a trail."

We have helped ourselves to data from too many sources to acknowledge our entire indebtedness here. However, special thanks are due Mr. Call McCarthy, for posing for pictures, and to the publishers of the *Chicago Tribune* for permission to reproduce here some of our contributions.

We will consider it a "good job" if it will induce the inexperienced to take up the delightful sport of bait casting or help the beginner over some rough spots, or contribute to the enjoyment of those already inoculated with the fever.

Anyway, here's wishing you some good strings.

LARRY ST. JOHN.

Chicago, August 1,
1917.

CONTENTS

PRACTICAL BAIT CASTING

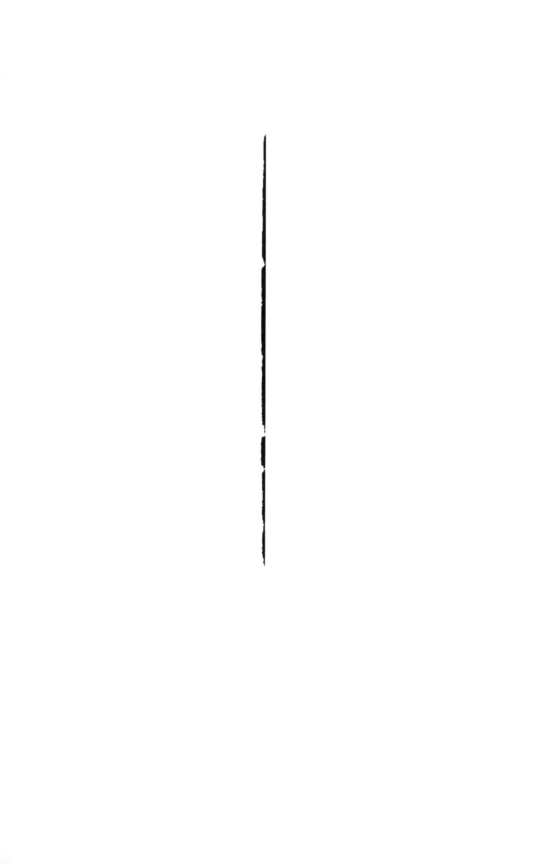

CHAPTER I

BAIT CASTING AS A MEANS OF CATCHING FISH

THE sun is rising and with it a breeze that drives the early morning mist away and gently ruffles the surface of the river.

On the shore, a still fisherman has just thrown out his line and he sprawls comfortably on the grassy bank, his freshly lighted pipe throwing out fragrant clouds of smoke.

Around the nearby bend comes a lone fisherman, wading the stream. He is dressed in waders and shooting jacket and carries a short casting rod. Now he stops and with skilful hand casts his lure—a spinner, red fly and strip of pork rind—into a likely-looking spot near the shore. Three casts he makes but with no results, so he goes on his way. Occasionally he stops where his practiced eye tells him there should be a fish, makes a few casts and then hurries along to another place.

Out in the stream near the still fisherman a rock juts its nose above the surface and approaching to within sixty feet of it the caster's rod goes back over his shoulder, then is whipped smartly but easily forward, sending the lure up, out, and then down. It strikes a few inches from the rock.

"That ought to——."

The remark is never finished. There is a mighty swirl, such as is made only by a fighting-mad, well-conditioned old "he-bass," the rod curves gracefully, and the battle is on.

For an instant the surprised fish permits himself to be reeled toward the fisherman. Then he turns and tries to regain the shelter of the big rock. The fisherman "gives him the butt," the rod bends dangerously near the limit, then the bass, as though suddenly changing his mind, dashes madly up stream, the line cutting the water in swift zigzags. Gradually this rush is stopped, and relentlessly he is reeled near the net. But no, the battle is not over! The fish leaps and madly endeavors to shake the hook from his mouth. With each leap the tautness of the line is maintained by a slight lifting of the rod, which is lowered as the fish re-enters the water. Finally he is led over the net and with a feeling of half-elation, half-regret, the fisherman removes the hook and places the game battler in his creel.

The fisherman continues his journey up stream. Now he stops near an identation in the shore line, known in angling parlance as a "pocket." Three or four casts produce nothing. At the next stop there is a swirl, a bass is hooked, but he leaps and frees himself. Farther on, near a fallen tree, a bass misses and a pickerel is creeled, and still farther another bass, but this ends the stream fishing, as the fisherman has now reached the lake of which the river is the outlet.

On the shore of the lake stands a boat-house. Unlocking the door, our friend enters and removes his waders. He gets into a large, flat-bottomed row-boat, gives the fly-wheel of the out-board motor a whirl, and goes "putt-putting" across the lake. At the end of the lake is a bed of lily pads and spatterdock and a weed-less hook and chunk of pork replaces the spinner, fly and strip. An hour's casting among these weeds scores two good, large mouth bass.

Now he heads out into the lake again, until he comes to a submerged weed bed. Here an artificial bait of the semi-surface type is used. The fisherman permits the boat to drift and makes short casts ahead of him, first to the extreme right, then diagonally out, and then straight ahead. The first trip over the bed produces a bass, so he tries it again with the same result. The third attempt is fishless, so once more he travels on.

This time, he goes to the other shore, near some islands, where the bottom is gravelly and there are numerous underwater rocky ledges—small mouth bass water.

The short rod is now given a rest, and a longer, lighter one put into service. The lure now is a live minnow, hooked through the lips, and it is cast with an easy sweeping side cast, so as not to jerk it from the

hook. The minnow is allowed to sink and then is
reeled in slowly.

One strike and a lost fish is the only result produced,
so blaming it on the time of day, the fisherman beaches
his boat, a cook kit is put to work, and soon the air is
laden with the scent of cooking fish and bacon, and
"bilin'" coffee—not at all unpleasant to the hungry
angler. After the "dishes are done" a pipe is lighted
and while the lines are drying an hour's rest is taken
in the shade of a willow tree.

Then the gravel bottom is given another trial, as this
fisherman has a pronounced fondness for small-mouth
bass. The first cast brings forth a hard strike, and a
ten-minute battle nets a specimen of a small-mouth bass
that would bring joy to any fisherman's heart, and two
hours more work produces two more bass and a pike-
perch of fair size. Another half hour of fishless effort
and the boat is headed toward the boathouse where
things are put in ship-shape order and the waders again
donned for the homeward journey down stream.

He does not fish so carefully now, because he considers that he has done a good day's "work"—his
catch now amounting to nine bass, one pickerel, and
one pike-perch. True he has not had one of those
red-letter days when the fish are "hittin' hard," when
three fish are often taken on three successive casts,
but on the other hand it was not one of those days, not
infrequent, when a day's casting produces not a single
strike.

He has caught cleanly and scientifically a fairly good string of fish, has been out in the open, has heard the birds sing and has seen the sunbeams dancing on the water—and it is just these things that lure men, and women too, from their daily tasks, that make up the play-work we call bait casting.

As he rounds the bend on his homeward journey, the still fisher hauls in his line, throws his string heavily laden with "sunnies" and perch over his shoulder, and wends his way homeward. Who can say which fisherman has had the more enjoyable day?

Writers on bait casting are inclined to compare their favorite sport with fly-casting, trolling, and other methods of fish taking, always, of course, to the disadvantage of the others, which is a grave mistake. Nothing we can say can detract from the beauties of fly-casting, the restfulness of trolling, or the opportunity of thinking things over and philosophizing when still fishing. To our way of thinking, all sportsman-like methods of fishing are legitimate; they all possess certain advantages and they all catch fish. Our advice to the youngster is to learn them all.

Bait casting, however, is second to no method as a means of catching fish for conditions that prevail over the greater part of the American continent. We do not recommend bait casting for taking trout, but for fishing for black bass and the members of the pike family in average American waters it has certain distinct and worth while advantages.

One of the merits of casting from the reel is the amount of water one can fish in a comparatively short time. For example, by anchoring his boat in the middle of a pool, one hundred and fifty feet in diameter, the caster can fish it all simply by casting 75 feet in each direction. Or when fishing from shore, he can easily fish 60 to 80 feet, up, down, and across the stream, without disturbing the water by wading or using a boat, or permitting the fish to suspect that one of the man-tribe is in the vicinity. Also by using weedless hooks he can fish in the weeds where it is often necessary to go in order to catch fish.

Besides the baits used in casting from the reel are of such a size that they are easily seen by the fish while they are in the air. One will realize the importance of this, if he will notice that the eyes of game fish, especially black bass, are placed near the top of their heads as they feed from the air as well as from the water. We have seen bass make a dash to get to a bait, while it is yet in the air, the same as an outfielder runs to get under a long fly. Furthermore, this sizeable bait makes a splash when it strikes the water which attracts the fish from a considerable distance and very often lures or angers them into striking.

Likewise the method of retrieving the bait, with the reel, permits regulating the speed and depth it travels to suit prevailing conditions. Finally, the mere mechanical process of casting a bait is pleasureable. As a youngster whom we taught to cast, puts it, "Its just as much fun to cast at a lily pad, or a projecting log, 25 yards away, as it is to shoot at a 4-inch bull, with a .22 at a hundred yards."

These advantages combined in one method explain its success as a means of catching fish, which in turn accounts for the fact that, although of comparatively recent origin, it is the most popular way of scientific angling now practiced in America.

Fly casting has been called the artistic man's recreation; still fishing the contemplative man's, but bait casting, with its continual moving about, is for the strenuous, although the sport is practiced successfully and enjoyed by people of limited energy.

CHAPTER II

LEARNING TO CAST

BAIT casting as practiced by an expert is an art combining remarkable accuracy, delicacy of thumbing, and at times great distances. To attain anything like perfection in bait casting requires years of experience and constant practice. Of course, the ability to drop one's lure within a few inches of a lily pad or rock is an advantage not to be underestimated; other things being equal, the most fish usually are on the string of the best caster.

Happily, however, it is not necessary to be a tournament caster for practical fish catching purposes. Good enough casting to catch fish under average conditions can be learned in a very short time, although it is hard to convince those who have tried it only once or twice that this is so. True, surprising things happen the first time one attempts to cast, but not more so than what happens to the beginner in skating or bicycle riding.

A few years ago, a friend was to accompany us on our vacation, and as he was not a caster we impressed upon him the advisability of learning the art. He was

THE OVERHEAD CAST

Whip the rod smartly and easily forward, slightly releasing the
pressure of the thumb on the reel as the rod passes the perpendicular. This movement is executed with the forearm and
wrist only.

somewhat skeptical, but the week before we were scheduled to leave town, he came to our home and we had a "session" out in the alley. In two hours he was casting fairly well at sixty and seventy feet, and with a few more hours' practice, in the evenings of the following week, he became quite proficient—proficient enough to make the writer exert himelf to keep a fish or two ahead of him during the next two weeks. Of course, he is one of those fellows who quickly "get the hang of things."

The best way to learn casting is to have some experienced caster act as teacher and coach—the rudiments can be learned in an hour or so, and the rest, of course, depends on the aptitude of the pupil and the amount of practice he devotes to the work.

In most of the larger cities, there are casting clubs which have casting pools in the public parks, and the person who wants to learn should go to one of these pools with his tackle. Here he will find plenty of capable teachers, who will gladly lend a hand, without charge, of course, because—well, just because the members of these clubs are invariably good fellows.

Lacking a tutor, the young angler must "pick it up" himself, which is not at all difficult, and we will try to offer here some helpful suggestions. Probably the best place to learn is a clear stretch of water without obstructions of any kind, but the majority of city anglers undoubtedly learned on a lawn or in an alley.

Grass or snow is preferable to bare ground on account of the wear the line gets on the latter.

The only tackle necessary in learning is a rod, a quadruple multiplying reel, a silk-line (preferably soft braid), and a weight of about ¾ of an ounce, which can be either a dipsey sinker or a minnow-shaped piece of wood. Later on the beginner can work down to the regulation ½ ounce and ¼ ounce tournament weights. If one learns by casting in water, let the weight be a regular artificial bait, either a surface bait or a wobbler, as these will float while back-lashes are being untangled.

Let us assume that the beginner is going to learn on the lawn. Let him peg down a newspaper forty feet away as a target, which should be left at that distance until he can hit it regularly.

The reel should be placed firmly in the reel seat on top of the rod. Some writers advise the beginner to place the reel down or on the bottom of the rod, but this is for a different style of casting (which we will deal with later on), consequently this warning may be necessary. See that the guides on the rod are all in a line, then run the line through each guide and out at the tip-top (top guide so called) and tie the weight to the end of the line.

The rod should be grasped firmly with all four fingers around the grip and the thumb pressed against the line on the reel. Some casters thumb the flange or spool-end of the reel instead of the line. The principal disadvantage of thumbing here is that the reel can be only partially filled with line, which tends to slow it up. The beginner is advised to learn to thumb the line and later, if he sees any advantage in thumbing the flange, he can easily change.

Reel the weight up to about nine inches from the tip of the rod. With the thumb firmly pressed on the spooled line, point the rod at the target. Now bring it straight back over the shoulder, the arms bending at the elbow, until the hand holding the rod is alongside the caster's right ear, and the tip pointing back, as shown in illustration. Now relax the wrist so it drops. You are now ready for the forward cast.

Whip the rod smartly forward, slightly releasing the pressure of the thumb on the reel as the rod passes the perpendicular. Keep the thumb on the line gently as the weight travels out. The first few attempts usually result in one or two things: The pressure exerted on the spool is too hard and the weight goes out only a few feet, or (more often) it is released altogether and the line runs from the reel faster than the bait can carry it out, resulting in what is commonly known as a "back lash." A description of this calamity would be superfluous in this chapter for beginners—anyone who has ever tried to cast can recognize a "back lash" without reading a description of it in a book.

Nothing but practice will teach the beginner how to thumb the reel properly. It is more or less of a knack and some pick it up more quickly than others, but if he is persistent, the beginner will soon find that his "back lashes" become beautifully less and less frequent although few casters ever are free from them entirely. The principal causes of back lashes are unevenly spooled lines and attempting to cast too far. The line must be felt by the thumb during the entire cast, and in attempting to throw his weight a great distance, the beginner unconsciously removes his thumb entirely from the reel, and, of course, a tangle is the result.

In the forward cast the rod is whipped forward smartly but easily, the speed increasing as the rod moves forward, the cast ending with a snap of the wrist, unless a very stiff rod is used, in which case a full arm swing is necessary. In making this forward cast, the rod is held so that the back of the hand and the handle of the reel are pointing almost straight up, the reason for this being that the line renders better through the guides with less danger of it clinging to the rod and because the reel runs more smoothly and easily in that position. At the finish of the cast, the thumb is clamped down tightly on the spool of the reel, and the rod is pointing upward at an angle of about 45 degrees.

As the forward cast is being made, the left hand is partially extended, and while the weight is still in the air, or the instant it lands, the rod is shifted to the left hand. The rear end of the reel is held in the palm of the left hand, the four fingers wrapped around the rod directly under the reel, and the thumb guides the line evenly on the reel. Usually the tension of the bait is sufficient; sometimes a slight downward pressure of the thumb, as it moves back and forth in front of the reel, is necessary.

Some people's hands are too small to hold the reel and rod comfortably in this position and they will find more pleasure in using the thumb and finger method of reeling. In this style, the rod is grasped directly in front of the reel with the last three fingers around the rod (some rods are provided with a forward grasp for this purpose) and the line is guided evenly on the reel, by the thumb and forefinger working back and forth in front of the reel

This guiding of the line on the reel must be done carefully at first, but later on it is performed almost unconsciously; it is important that it be done, however, as an unevenly wound line is one of the very worst breeders of "back-lashes."

When the weight strikes the ground the caster "follows through" with rod until it is pointing at or a trifle above the target. The rod is then kept pointing directly at the weight while the latter is being reeled in. We advise this in spite of the fact that many of the older, and very able, casters retrieve their bait with the rod pointing almost straight up. Our reasons for so advising are stated in another chapter.

The beginner should practice casting at his target at forty feet for some time—say until he can hit it three out of four casts. Then he can move it up another ten feet. We cannot urge the novice too strongly on this point, as we know the temptation to cast for distance is great, but he must keep in mind these facts: Accuracy is the very foundation of a bait caster's education; distance will follow naturally. Very few casts over sixty or seventy feet are made in actual fishing and, as Samuel Camp remarks: "The man who tries to cast 'clean across' the lake usually gets more exercise than fish." The man who can drop his lure where he wants to is a better and more successful fisherman, always, than he who can cast far but with only a general idea as to where his bait is going to strike.

The cast described above is the "over-the-shoulder" or "overhead" cast. It possesses several advantages over other styles. It it far more accurate (all tournament casters use this method) and there is less danger of hooking your companions when fishing with more than one in a boat. The side caster, if he is right-handed, must always be placed in the right end of the boat and this is sometimes an inconvenience.

It seems to be the general idea that the "overhead" cast is harder to learn, but this is not so. It is so easy to master as the other casts, and should be learned first by all means. The others are simply modifications of the overhead and are easily learned once you know that style.

In the side cast, or "side-swipe" as it is sometimes called, the rod is brought back to the right side of the body, parallel with the water, and is then whipped forward. It is useful when fishing over the end of a boat or from the banks of a stream where there are branches or other obstructions that prevent overhead casting. It is not so "jerky" as the overhead and consequently does not put so much strain on the line. It is also restful after hard and persistent overhead casting.

The underhand cast is made by bringing the right arm across the body so that the rod is on the left side, the rod tip pointing slightly downward. It is then swept out and across the body again to the right, the pressure being slightly released on the spool of the reel when the rod is pointing almost straight ahead. This cast is not practiced much with the short rod, and is explained further under the heading "Casting with the Henshall rod."

A cast which we might call the "lift" is sometimes made from the shore, when standing on the deck of a boat or from a dock or pier. The rod is pointed down and a little to the rear of the right-hand side of the body, the hand being about at the hip. The rod is then smartly lifted up and out, and the cast finished with the hand about on a level with the eyes. This cast will be found useful in working against a strong wind wherever it is possible to cast standing up. It drops a bait very nicely.

Summary

Reel the weight to about nine inches from the tip; grasp rod firmly with thumb on spooled line. Point rod at the target. Bring rod straight over the shoulder, back far enough to bring the reel on a level with right ear. Drop wrist. Make forward cast straight at target, slower at first, accelerating speed as you go. When rod is little past perpendicular release thumb pressure some, but not entirely, from reel. Hold rod so that the back of hand and reel handle point upwards. Finish cast with forward snap of wrist. Shift rod to left hand. Point rod directly at the weight. Reel in, guiding line on reel evenly.

CASTING FOR FISH

FOR ADVANCED PUPILS

After the novice has tried his hand at dry land casting, he becomes anxious to test his skill on real fish, which is a natural and laudable ambition.

One of the first things to be learned in actual fishing. is to cast sitting down—not at all difficult. Casting standing up is hard work, is dangerous in anything but a mud scow, and besides when the water is smooth and clear one must cast farther to prevent being seen by the fish as a fisherman standing in a boat is outlined against the sky and looks like the proverbial "house afire" to the fish.

One of the troubles experienced by new casters is casting on too direct a line—"shooting the bait" it is called. To overcome this, cast at an imaginary spot above and behind the place you want to strike, and stop your bait as it goes over. Lengthening the amount of line between the bait and the rod tip before casting should cause your bait to travel higher. If it doesn't the pressure on the spooled line is not released soon enough. In this connection, avoid reeling your bait up too close to the tip as the metal part of the lure may crack the agate lining of the tip top. Before casting, be sure that the line is not wrapped around the tip, or you may throw your whole outfit overboard.

One thing the young caster will learn as he progresses is that in actual fishing, a hard cast is not needed to get a reasonable amount of line out—just a slight movement of the arm and wrist. Snapping the wrist backwards when bringing the rod over the shoulder instead of merely relaxing it will help to put the spring of the rod in the cast. Hard straight arm casting defeats its purpose, because as you increase the power of your cast, you must likewise increase the thumb pressure on the reel or spend time that should be devoted to fishing in untangling a snarled line. Cast with the wind behind you whenever possible.

One of the most important things in casting for fish is to retrieve the bait quickly—it should be started back before, or the very instant, it strikes the water. This is done by aiming over and behind the target, as mentioned before, and stopping the bait suddenly, which takes up all slack line. It should be helped by a slight twitch of the rod to one side. This is done usually when the rod is shifted to the left hand. This quick retrieve is something the novice should practice diligent-ly—it means more strikes and more fish.

CASTING WITH THE HENSHALL ROD

Scientific bait casting originated with the Henshall rod (discussed in the chapter on rods), which is usually 8¼ feet long. Live bait is nearly always used with this style of fishing. This method has much to recommend it, although it is not practiced as much as former¬ly, due to the overwhelming popularity of the short rod. Neverthleess, there is no denying that the old style casting and Henshall rod have their advantages. The older men who use them can lay down a long line with remarkable accuracy and they catch their share of fish.

The same reel and line are employed as with casting with the short rod, but the reel is placed in the reel seat so that the handle is toward the left when on top of the rod. The cast is made with the reel on top, but when the rod is shifted to the left hand, it is turned so that the reel is beneath the rod with the handle to the right. In casting to the left the movements are as follows:

The angler stands facing the front, but his head is turned toward the spot he is casting at. The rod is pointed downward and to the right. It is then swept out and across the body upwards, the hand traveling from the right hip to the left shoulder.

In casting to the right, the movements are reversed —the rod arm crossing the body from the left hip to a level with the right shoulder. In both casts, the body is swung slightly with the casting arm, so that the movement is steady and without a jerk at the end of the cast.

When the bait strikes the water, the rod is shifted to the left hand, and rolled over so the handle is to the right, the bait reeled in and the line guided evenly on the spool.

STRIP CASTING

This style of fishing is also called "slack-line" casting, or Greenwood Lake casting from the New Jersey lake where it is practiced extensively. For this, either a Henshall pattern rod, or a heavy, rather stiff fly-rod is used. An enameled line, as heavy as the rod can handle, such as is used in fly-casting, is the most satisfactory, as it is less likely to kink, and its large diameter makes it easy to manipulate with the hand.

The reel is used simply to hold surplus line, so it can be of any kind; usually a large, single action click reel is employed. The baits commonly used in bait casting such as large minnows, frogs, pork, or artificials are all successful with this method. Strip casting can be done either from a boat or when wading but is usually a boat proposition.

Line equalling the length of the rod is pulled through the tip and sufficient line to reach the desired spot is then pulled from the reel, between the reel and the first guide, and allowed to fall at the caster's feet in loose coils in the bottom of the boat or on the shore. The bait is then swung out, pendulum-fashion, straight ahead by lifting and swinging the rod, the coiled line running through the fingers of the left hand. The outgoing line is stopped by the fingers and then you proceed as in casting a fly. That is, the rod is pointed straight out parallel with the water and all slack is taken up with the left hand. Then the rod is swung back straight over the shoulder and the bait allowed to strike straight behind. As soon as it strikes (you can feel and hear it), it is cast forward again. The forward cast is made straight over the shoulder. Push hard with the thumb and use plenty of wrist action.

As the bait starts forward, the line held in the left hand is permitted to run out between the fingers, but is stopped as soon as the bait strikes the water. The bait is then retrieved by pulling in the line with the left hand, the rod being held parallel with the water again for quick striking. The fish is played by manipulating the line with the left hand and not with the reel. This, together with a spring of the long rod, gives the angler complete control over a hooked fish.

When fishing from shore the bait can seldom be cast behind the angler, but the forward cast is started as soon as the bait "pulls" from behind.

The "side swipe" is also employed in strip casting, not so much line being pulled through the tip top of the rod but otherwise the cast is the same except, of course, the rod is swung to one side instead of straight back.

It will be seen that strip casting is a cross between bait and fly casting, and is very effective under certain conditions. The best places to use this style of fishing, are large quiet streams, shallow flats, protected bays, or extensive feeding grounds, especially when the fish are feeding on the surface and are rising readily to the splash of heavy baits. A skillful strip caster can cover an immense amount of water as he can make three or four casts to one made by casting from the reel.

SUMMARY

For accuracy and safety, overhead casting. This should be learned first.

For casting against heavy wind or where accuracy is not necessary, or for a rest from overhead casting, side casting.

For casting from shore where back-cast is impossible, under-hand casting.

For casting from deck of boat or dock, especially against wind, "lift" casting.

For casting in open water and with live bait, use Henshall rod with side or under-hand cast.

For casting to cover the greatest amount of water in the shortest time, strip casting.

CHAPTER III

THE ROD

FITTINGS, style, length and weight, material and price, are the things usually considered in choosing a casting rod. They are all related, yet if we were to combine the very best characteristic of each in one rod the result would not be an ideal tool for all kinds of casting. Such a rod would possess the limitations of any Jack-of-All-Trades. In other words, there is no such thing as an ideal all-around rod.

Obviously the rod suitable for casting plugs weighing an ounce must be fairly stiff and heavy; so must the rod that will be used for fishing in heavy weed growth or in other places where the fish must be brought to gaff quickly or never, and where the "derricking" of weeds is inevitable even with the most weedless of hooks. On the other hand, for casting light spinners or pork strip weighing a quarter of an ounce or so you will need, for the best work, a rod with considerable "whip." The same rod would give you more sport in open water fishing. So in buying a rod, besides the features mentioned above, we must also consider the kinds of bait we will use, the places we will fish, and the kind and size of fish we are likely to try conclusions with.

FITTINGS

In the fittings of the rod we may cater to our whims somewhat, because if they do not suit us we can easily replace them with some that do, with the possible exception of ferrules. True, most rods are used just as they come from the shop, but refitted rods are by no means rare.

The ferrules are the principal fittings and the wise angler is careful to find out what he is getting in this line when buying a rod. Ferrules are made either of brass, nickel-plated, or of German silver. The oxidized finish often seen on English fly rods is desirable and we wonder why it is not used more in this country. German silver is the best ferrule material and for those used on the higher grade rods the metal is drawn and redrawn until it has the temper of steel. Also care is used in designing a good ferrule so that it is not necessary to cut away any of the wood to get a good fit.

Good ferrules are "welted." That is, the open end of the female half is reinforced by an extra piece—welt—of metal, and they are "capped" or shouldered to insure a perfect union of wood and metal. Good bamboo rods nowadays seldom have anything but serrated ferrules, (a few makers have perfected ferrules of their own that are excellent but we are referring now to the ferrules found in the average tackle store) as each tooth fits on a face of a strip of the bamboo, making it more flexible than the solid tube type and therefore reduces the stiffness at the joints, always the ear-marks of a cheap rod. Furthermore, good ferrules are waterproofed by having a bottom or partition instead of being simply a tube. This protects the ends of the wood from moisture and possible rotting.

Beware of extremely long ferrules, and if possible avoid those fastened with a pin as it will be troublesome when you overhaul the rod, which will eventually have to be done.

Grasps or Handles

The hand grasp should be of solid cork, either in one piece or better of cork discs or washers over a core of wood. Next in desirability is the cane wound handle; then the celluloid wound; then the solid wood, and last the cork veneer. The shape is a matter of personal preference, although one with a knob or flare at the butt will prevent the rod slipping from your hand, especially very early or very late in the season when your otherwise "trusty right" may be numb with cold.

The rod may be equipped with either single or double grasp. In the double style there is a small forward grasp, or winding grip, in front of the reel seat. It adds but little weight to the rod, rests the hand, and prevents cramped fingers, especially if you use the thumb and finger method of laying the line on the spool.

REEL SEAT AND OTHER MOUNTINGS

The reel seat, butt cap, taper, and reel bands should be of German silver as this material soon loses its flashiness, which is a decided advantage, without looking disreputable. Cheap rods are always nickel mounted.

With the reel seat there is included the reel bands to keep the reel from falling off. With a fly rod simple rings are adequate, but in bait casting the reel is thumbed and there is danger of pushing the reel into the water. We prefer the hood on the front of the reel seat, so that the reel is seated from behind, which prevents it being pushed off in thumbing.

Since the finger hook has gone out of style many reel locking devices have been brought out, but many of them are failures. We rather like the finger hook. It rests the hand and it is a sure guard against pushing the reel off. Probably the best little "trick" is the detachable finger hook. It can be carried in the tackle box and the rod can be used alternately with and without it which is the best way we know of preventing "caster's cramp." Another device worthy of special mention is the Huffman Attachment. This is a combination finger hook, reel lock, and hand rest.

A fitting of special merit is the detachable rubber butt, particularly if you reel with the butt of the rod resting against your six feet, more or less, of virile young manhood as the novels say. Its cost, twenty-five cents, is not much to gamble and its "comfiness" may pleasantly surprise you.

GUIDES

There are many different styles of guides, but not all of them are suitable for bait casting. The German silver trumpet guides were once the most popular, but with the advent of the short rod they were driven out, temporarily, by the exaggerated Kalamazoo pattern— often as large as a silver quarter. The tendency now is toward medium size guides, either trumpet, bell, or casting ring with off-set tip-top, which is the English term for the tip guide and prevents confusion with the tip proper.

German silver or hardened steel is used throughout on the lower priced rods, the rods of the better class being fitted with guides and tip-top lined with agate, or imitation agate. Agate reduces the friction to a minimum—it saves wear on the line as well as on the guide itself. Soft metal guides eventually become roughened, which quickly plays havoc with the line. Most of the friction, however, comes at the first, or hand guide and at the tip-top and these at least should be of agate or glass, even on cheap rods. The hardened steel guides are much harder, and therefore better than those of German silver.

Too many guides should be avoided as they tend to retard the line, but they should be close enough together to make the line follow the curve of the rod when a strain is put on it. Guides too far apart permit the line to jump directly from one guide to the next, putting too much strain at one place on the line and rod.

WINDINGS

Windings are put on a rod to hold the pieces together, in case of a split rod, and they have some effect on the rod's action; also they are ornamental. Most rods have the winding put on in clusters at intervals along the rod, and this style seems to answer the purpose very well. Sometimes they are wound diagonally or diamond-shaped, the theory being that they make the rod stronger. Our experience with spiral wound rods is limited so we are unable to say whether or not they are an improvement on the clusters.

Some rods are wrapped solid the entire length which no doubt produces a rod of enormous strength, but the "solid silk" rods we have used have the "smooth" action of a good wood rod rather than of bamboo. Color of windings is a matter of personal taste.

STYLE

In determining the style of rod we have two things to consider: Action or casting efficiency and convenience or portability, the latter hinging more on the kinds of fishing trips taken than on anything else. The one-piece rod is unequalled in action because it is "ferrul-less" and it is a well-known fact that a ferrule, being a more or less unyielding piece of metal binding a resilient piece of wood, impairs the action of the rod. This is especially true of cheap rods because the quality of the ferrule is poor.

However, the one-piece rod is inconvenient to carry. One measuring five feet requires a case sixty-two inches long which is an awkward thing to carry on week-end trips possibly on crowded street cars, trains, busses, and other conveyances.

For the man having a permanent camp or some fishing place where he leaves his tackle during the season or the lucky fellow living but a short distance from his fishing "grounds" the one-piece style is unreservedly recommended. Practically the same may be said of the one-piece rod with independent handle. The caster using a one-piece rod should bear in mind the fact that he has no extra tip to fall back on if an accident occurs. The user of a one-piece rod should know how to "splice."

The two-piece style with the ferrule in the middle of the rod is not as weak as painted, because, as a matter of fact, the ferrule is not in the center of the rod from the fishing standpoint, the leverage being exerted from in front of the grasp. However, the action of this type of rod is none too good and few high-grade rods are now being made in this way.

The two-piece rod with short butt and long tip is a good style. This type, we believe, solves satisfactorily the problem of good, unobstructed action combined with portability. The tip is usually about thirty-five inches long—not at all hard to carry—and the ferrule is located far enough down to be in the heavy part of the rod, where there is not a great deal of action anyway, and much below the vulnerable middle where the strain comes. These rods possess plenty of casting force and speed and we confess a partiality for them. Note that most good salt water rods are of this type.

If you "tote" a large suit case with you on your fishing trips the three-piece rod is easier to carry—otherwise its shorter joints are not worth the extra ferrule because a thirty-six inch case is just as easy to carry as one two feet in length. Some of the very highest priced rods are made in the three-piece style and there is no denying that they are strictly first-class in every respect. As a word of warning, however, the short butt, long tip construction is miles ahead of the three-piece in the low and medium priced grades. Of course, the steel rod, not being made generally in the two-piece style, is not included in the above comparison because the steel rod's ferrules are a part of the rod itself and while thickened at the joints a trifle, they do not interfere with the rod's action as do ferrules in a bamboo or wood rod.

It is sometimes necessary, as on an extended canoe trip, for example, to minimize on weight and space and that is the only excuse for the "combination" rods. In a few cases they are well-made rods costing as much as twenty-five dollars, but at their best they are only makeshifts, as is to be expected. One model—and this describes them all as a class—consists of six pieces; a reversible handle and two joints, making a nine and a half foot fly rod with extra tip and the handle and two other joints produce a five foot casting rod.

Personally, we favor the steel telescope rod with reversible handle for a double-purpose rod. By this we mean the kind that has the guides on the outside and not the one with the line running through the center. Such a rod with agate guides costs from four to six dollars, can be telescoped to three feet, and can be used any length from that to eight feet.

Suit case, "Sunday," or pocket rods consisting of four or more pieces are designed to meet the demand for a very compact, easy-to-carry rod and answer the purpose very well. They are especially valuable to salesmen, motor-cyclists, and others traveling through territory where there is good fishing, who do not care to depend upon borrowed tackle or on the "rods" furnished by the man who rents the boats and sells the minnows.

Length and Weight

The original casting rods as used in the early part of the last century by the good folks who originated the Kentucky reel were from twelve to fifteen feet in length. Along in the seventies Dr. Henshall, good and true sportsman, brought out the rod bearing his name, which was eight and a quarter feet long. This rod and the Doctor's writings put the black bass on the map. Of course, the Henshall rod, because of its length is used with the under-hand cast with live bait.

That it possesses some advantage over the shorter rod is obvious. It is unequalled for casting live bait, as the smoother action prevents snapping the minnow from the hook or whipping the life out of a frog and there is no reason why it cannot be used with the lighter artificial baits. It is a general purpose rod, fine for still fishing, trolling, etc. Every fisherman should have one.

Nevertheless, the short rod possesses merits all its own and it is here to stay. The short rod has had much abuse heaped upon it. Dr. Henshall himself accuses the man who uses one of being a "pot" fisherman. No doubt the short rod, when the Doctor wrote his excellent book, "The Book of the Black Bass" was a stiff, inartistic affair, but this cannot be said of the short rods as they are made to-day. They are just as fine in their way as are fly rods or bait rods.

The modern, short casting rod originated some time in the nineties in the vicinity of Chicago to meet fishing conditions in the Middle West—Wisconsin, Illinois, Michigan, and Indiana particularly—where there are thousands of small, weedy lakes requiring accurate casting and therefore the overhead cast, and its popularity was assured when heavy artificial baits came into general use, as the short rod is the only one that can handle lures of this type. The first short rods ranged from three and a half to six and a half feet in length, but as the sport grew experience showed that rods from four and a half to six and a quarter feet were the most practical, five feet being the average.

In casting rods, as in many other things, we bump into the necessity of sacrificing one advantage to gain another. The shorter rods are more efficient casting tools; the longer ones more efficient fishing tools. It is axiomatic that the longer the rod the more certainty of hooking a rising fish, the more control you have over him after he is hooked, and the more pleasure you have in landing him. On the other hand, the short rods are better for distance and accuracy—it is very hard work to cast overhead with rods over six and a quarter feet long.

Weight depends a great deal on material and construction. As a general rule bamboo averages about one ounce per foot in length; solid wood, fifteen to twenty per cent heavier; steel thirty to fifty per cent, although makers of steel rods are making them lighter than formerly and at least one model is now on the market that is about as light as bamboo.

Weight in ounces is rather misleading. A six foot bamboo rod will weigh about 6¼ ounces, but its action may be either stiff or "whippy" in the tip and therefore action as well as weight must be considered. We quote from a catalogue to illustrate the variations in some standard rods: Bamboo, length 5 feet, light, 5 ounces; standard 5½ ounces; heavy, 6 ounces. Five feet six inches, light, 5¼ ounces; standard 5¾ ounces; heavy, 6 ounces. Six feet, light, 6 ounces; standard 6½ ounces,; heavy, 6¾ or 7 ounces; lancewood, length 5 feet, light, 5¾ ounces; standard 6¼ ounces; steel 5 feet and five feet six inches, average weight 8 ounces.

MATERIALS AND PRICES

When the short rod first came into use much experimenting was done with different materials. Rods with ash or hickory butts and lancewood or cane tips were common. Later on osage orange and other woods were popular.

The materials now commonly used in making casting rods are steel, the solid woods, like noibwood, bethabara, dagama, greenheart, lancewood, and split bamboo.

We do not share many angler-writers' prejudice against steel as a casting-rod material. Bait casting, as generally practiced, is a strenuous sport and requires sturdy tools. Steel has its advantages as well as drawbacks. It is heavy but strong, lacking the nicest balance, but requires little care; its action is not as resilient as that of bamboo, but then its ferrules do not come loose and rattle if kept in a steam-heated room where many rods must be stored between seasons. In short, the once-in-a-while fisherman who intends to buy one rod will make no mistake in getting one of steel. They make good knockabout rods for any caster, no matter how many fine bamboo or wood rods he may possess.

Steel rods are especially recommended for use where heavy fish predominate such as certain northern muskie and pike waters or in Southern States where the bass run very large. Of course, in recommending steel rods we refer only to the best grade which is guaranteed.

The steel rod was a long time in coming. Early experiments with the tubular steel rods showed that they would not withstand a twisting motion or side strain. Finally this difficulty was overcome by making the rod in tubular form, but not brazing the edges together.

The medium grades are fair, but the cheap steel rods, and the market is flooded with them, are to be avoided even more than cheap bamboo. The average model in a good grade, equipped with German silver guides and agate tip-top, retails at about $5.00. The light weight construction, with same fitting, at $6.00, and depending upon the quality of fittings such as all

agate guides, double grips, etc., the prices run up to
$10.00.

The quality of wood rods depends a great deal on
the closeness of grain and other characteristics of the
pieces used in making individual rods, but as a general
thing the different woods rank in merit in about the
order we have named them at the beginning of this
chapter.

As a general rule wood rods lack the snappy, thor-
oughbred action of bamboo and they are heavier; they
excel steel in this respect, but require more care. Some
mighty nice rods are made of solid wood. Their action
might be described by the word "smooth," and for
fairly heavy work or general fishing many experienced
anglers prefer them above all others. Prices vary,
but a first-class rod in the various woods, comes about
as follows: Noibwood, thirteen dollars; bethabara and
dagama, ten dollars; greenheart, nine dollars; lancewood, seven dollars. Two dollars should be added
to these prices for agate first guide and tip-top.

Tournament casters are unanimously in favor of
split bamboo, but practical fishermen are not agreed on
its all-round superiority. It has some real disadvant-
ages, viewed from the angler's standpoint, such as the
necessity of overhauling, and sometimes practically re-
building every year or so, which to some is work and
to others play. Those who look at it in the latter
light, of course, do not hesitate to select bamboo.

Undoubtedly it has resiliency, snap, go, "pep," or whatever you want to call it; also that hard-to-describe-quality we call balance in greater degree than any other material. Likewise it is lighter in proportion to length and strength than wood or steel, and viewed merely from the standpoint of casting and fishing efficiency, it is without an equal.

Parenthetically, a light bamboo rod is not recommended for fishing regularly, where large pickerel or pike predominate, as their dead weight and underwater style of fighting break down the fiber of bamboo and will eventually "put a set" in the best of tips.

Coming to the subject of how much to pay for a rod, let us first turn our attention to the time-worn statement that if you cannot afford to invest from $25.00 to $30.00 in a bamboo rod, it is better to pay from $12.00 to $18.00 for one of solid wood. Years ago this statement may have been true; it is not true to-day. At any rate it does not apply to the casting rod. For a fly-rod fairly long pieces of small diameter and considerable strength are required and this kind of bamboo is becoming rare. Besides not nearly so high an order of workmanship is necessary in making a short rod—witness the fact that you probably know any number of men who make their own casting rods but buy their fly rods. Furthermore, because of the popularity of bamboo short rods, more attention has been paid by manufacturers to the problem of producing them for little money—this is the twentieth century!

As a matter of fact you can buy a casting rod of a well-known make for less than $2.00 that is really a wonderful production for the money. Of course, the fittings are not high grade, but it is an efficient little rod just the same.

A fairly good bamboo casting rod can be bought for from $6.00 to $9.00. Such a rod will be nickel mounted, of course, but it will probably be fitted with an agate first guide and a tip-top, and in the two-piece style a German silver ferrule. Its action will be fair, especially for a "stiffish" rod, and it will stand a lot of hard service. For from $10.00 to $15.00, you can get a rod good enough for anyone. It will be German silver mounted throughout, with agate guides and tip-top, extra tip, and solid cork handle, and will be a satisfactory rod in every respect.

The $25.00 and $30.00 rods are veritable works of art, being hand-made of the very best materials, beautiful in action and leave nothing to be desired in the way of casting efficiency. The experienced caster would probably be wise in buying a rod of this kind if he can afford the expenditure. In buying a rod, however, keep this fact in mind: The rod plays a minor part in bait casting. It is not nearly so important as the reel and line. Therefore if you must economize do it on the rod. The beginner, regardless of his bank account, will do better with a medium-priced rod until he learns what he wants.

Of course, we assume that you know that bamboo

is not used just as it comes from the jungle. Only the best pieces can be put in good rods, and 'these are first split and glued together to reduce the diameter and at the same time utilize the strength of the hard outer surface or enamel—hence the term split bamboo. Usually the six strip construction is employed, which no doubt is to be preferred since most good rods are made that way. The wood is split and then fitted together very similar to the way the sections of a peeled orange fit.

A few high grade rods are made in the eight strip style, and their makers claim for them superior action owing to the rod being nearer a true cylinder, but the difference is too small to be of any consequence, while the tips may be poor because of the amount of glue necessary to hold the slender pieces together. However, if you want a round rod get the eight strip—beware of the six strip planed down as this trimming is likely to weaken the rod.

There are several varieties of bamboo, but all of them cannot be used in making good split rods. The Chinese and Japanese canes are strong and resilient, but the joints are too short and they are therefore used only in the natural state for the common "cane poles."

Calcutta is no doubt the best bamboo, but Calcutta is almost impossible to obtain. In fact, according to Perry Frazer, a recognized authority, it is so rare that we may as well forget it. Calcutta comes in two varities, female and male, and the latter is preferable because the female of the species is weaker than the male. It is usually mottled by being burned to re-move "suckers" or side growth, or for sheer ornamenta-tion. Tonkin, however, is often stained to imitate this burned effect. The bamboo used to-day is the Tonkin. It is stiffer than Calcutta, and for this reason is usually preferred by tournament casters. It differs from Calcutta in having smaller nodes and is seldom burned.

The idea of splitting cane or wood and then gluing it together is of English origin, but the split bamboo rod as we know it, was invented by Samuel Phillipe, according to Dr. Henshall, who gives the date of his first rod as 1844. Regardless of who conceived the idea, American bamboo rods are quite in a class by themselves as regards workmanship.

SUMMARY

FITTINGS

Best ferrules: German silver, serrated, capped, water-proofed, welted.

Best mountings: German silver. Best Guides: All agate, narrow casting and off-set tip-top. Next best: Agate, first guide and tip-top. Third best: Steel ring guides and off-set tip-top.

STYLE

Best action. Least convenient; one piece construc-tion.

Next best action.   More convenient: Two piece, short butt, long tip construction.

More convenient. Slightly poorer action; Three piece construction.

Most convenient. Poorest action; Rods of four or more pieces.

LENGTH

Finest action.   For light lures and open water, 6 or 6¼ feet.

Poorer action.   For heavy baits and obstructed water, 4½ to 5 feet.

General purpose: 5 to 6 feet.

MATERIAL

Best action.   Requires more care: Bamboo.   Poorer action.   Less care: solid wood.   Poorest action. Least care: steel.

Looking at this summary, we find many conflicting points.   So many, in fact, that an all-round rod is—well, "there's no sech animile."   However, as a summary sort of pins a fellow down to say something, here's what we would choose if some cruel fate would compel us to keep only one rod.

If we fished but a few times a season: steel, 5½ feet long; agate first guide and tip-top.

If we fished habitually: 6 strip bamboo; 5½ feet long; two pieces short butt, long tip style; otherwise same as above.

Local conditions often influence the choice of a rod.

The ideal condition is to have and use, except when wading a stream of course, two rods. Carry both of them in the boat with you, rigged ready for action. One could be of steel or wood—say 5 feet in length, for use with a fairly heavy line; just the combination for weedy, littered-up water, heavy fish, or the larger bait. The other could be more on the "buggy whip" order. Let it be of bamboo, 6 or 6¼ feet long to be used in open water fishing, with the lighter lures and a light line.

HOME MADE RODS

It is no reflection on the casting rod to say that it is neither as expensive nor as difficult to make as a fly rod.

Many casters make their own rods and for the man "handy with tools" it is not a great deal of labor and an enjoyable and profitable pastime between seasons.

Bamboo, making as it does such a nice rod, will naturally be the first choice as to the material of most beginners in rod making. Probably it is a good plan to get the pieces of bamboo all glued up so that the "making" of the rod is simply a matter of fitting the joints, putting on handle, mountings, and guides, and then winding and varnishing. Bamboo of this kind is catalogued by big tackle dealers as "unmounted split bamboo" and it comes usually in two or three grades. What grade to buy depends on the confidence of the man who is going to do the work. This work will give the beginner some ideas on the subject and then he can graduate into actual rod making.

As one good solid rod is needed by every caster it is best to start on this material and we would recommend either bethabara, dagama, or greenheart.

Bethabara or washaba, as it is sometimes called, is a good rod material. It is hard, close grained, and in appearance is similar to light walnut. To avoid substitution, it should be bought only from reliable sources. Usually it is furnished "in square" in four, five, and six feet lengths, one-half, three-fourths, and one inch square, and the rod maker must "work it down."

Dagama is also a good wood for the beginner. It comes from Cuba and resembles lancewood in color but makes a much better rod and is easy to work with or against the grain.

After the beginner has worked with solid wood he may attempt to make a split bamboo rod, although few amateurs ever reach that point, as it is so convenient to buy the glued pieces. There are a number of pitfalls for the beginner in rod making and the man attempting his first rod is advised to read "The Amateur Rod-Maker" by Perry D. Frazer. Mr. Frazer is not a professional and there are no doubt better rod makers than he, but few who know, as he knows, the troubles of the beginner and how to avoid them with a minimum of expense.

THE CARE OF THE ROD.

The steel rod's chief virtue is that it needs little

care. Rust is its worst enemy and this can be guarded
against by carrying a rag, or better still, a piece of
chamois skin saturated with oil and wiping off the
rod before putting it away. This and a drop of oil
on the ferrules, once in a while, is usually all the
care necessary with a steel rod. The best grades
have a number of coats of good enamel baked on
which is very durable. As soon as it begins to show
signs of wear, it should be touched up with bicycle
enamel.

Dry rot is the thing to avoid with wood rods and
they should be kept well varnished at all times; otherwise the heat will warp or set the tip.

Bamboo rods should also be protected by varnish
and they should not be stored near heat as it shrinks
the bamboo and consequently the ferrules rattle and
come loose.

At the end of every season the bamboo rods
should be gone over and all frayed wrappings replaced,
the varnish rubbed down with a little oil and pumice,
and the whole rod given one or two coats of good varnish. Varnish should be applied with a bristle brush,
the varnish should be slightly warmed, and the work
done in a warm room. The rod should be dried by
hanging where dust cannot get at it.

Varnish not only affects the life of the rod, but its
action as well; it makes it proof against moisture, and
the effects of change in temperature to which unpro-
tected bamboo is very sensitive. Bamboo casting rods

should never be used for trolling unless kept pointing at the bait so the strain is on the line, nor for still fishing. Neither should they be left lying on the ground nor any place else without support for the tip. To stand a rod in the corner and then go away and leave it there is not good for the rod.

Every permanent camp should have a good place to keep the rods. The best place at a resort for a rod not in use is in its case, or, if assembled, under the bed; the best place at home, is suspended in a cool room. In the average city home, the top shelf of the pantry is a good place if the rod is kept in its case, as this room is usually kept cool. Avoid if possible, a set in the tip; to cure one the best thing to do is to suspend it by the tip-top and tie a small weight on the lower end.

Every time the rod is used it should be wiped dry before being put away and the tip should be straightened carefully with the hands. The idea of using tips alternately is a good one, as the tip joint not in use can be hung up to straighten. In putting a three piece rod together start at the tip and work down, joining the butt last. In taking the rod apart reverse this order and remove tip last. Rub the ferrules along side of nose or in the hair to lubricate them when putting the rod together. If the ferrule sticks do not twist or wrench it. Get some one to help you and pull straight, grasping the ferrule as far down as possible. Be very careful about filing down tight ferrules. If it must be done it is better to take it to a tackle shop unless you are sure of your ability to do it properly.

A stick of ferrule cement, a little winding silk, and a small bottle of varnish and brush make a good simple repair kit. The addition of an extra guide or so and a tip-top will help. The regular repair kits are also desirable.

Every user of a steel rod should carry in the tackle box one or two of the emergency tips.

ROD CASES.

In buying a case get one that will hold at least two rods as it is as easy to carry as a one-rod case and you should have an emergency outfit with you whenever possible.

Our favorite case is forty-two inches long. By taking the rods from their forms and putting them in a partitioned roll of light khaki we can carry two bait rods and two fly rods with extra tips or, leaving out one rod, we can find room for a landing net frame and handle. The practice of carrying a rod strapped to a suitcase is likely to result in a smashed rod some time. A rod case—stiff enough to protect the rods—will be found a good investment.

CHAPTER IV

THE REEL

THE reel is the most important part of the bait caster's outfit—it is the part that does most of the actual work. The amount of this work sometimes is terrific—six or eight hours continuously of casting and retrieving on "hard" days. The reel for bait casting must be free running and geared so its action is sustained for a considerable period. Although a few 3-ply reels are used, the quadruple multiplier is the favorite. In a quadruple multiplying reel the spool revolves four times to one turn of the handle, this being obtained by the number of teeth in the driving gear and the pinion.

Mechanically, the multiplying reel is very simple, considering the work it accomplishes. There is a small gear, the pinion, on the end of the spool shaft or "hub," which engages with the gearing of the wheel or driving gear attached to the shaft of the handle. Depending on this gearing, the spool turns two, three, or four times, making a double, triple, or quadruple multiplying reel. For example, ten teeth in the pinion and forty in the driving gear would give four turns of the spool to one of the handle.

THUMBING THE REEL

In making the cast the back of the hand and the reel handle should point almost straight up, the thumb pressing evenly to control the running of the line.

SPOOLING THE LINE WITH THUMB ONLY

This is the usual method. Hold the rear end of the reel in the palm of the left hand and guide the line on the reel with a slight downward pressure of the thumb.

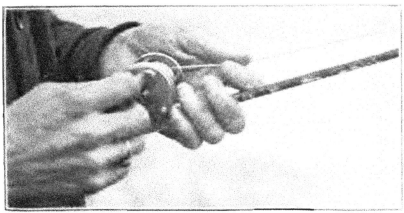

THUMB AND FINGER SPOOLING

If the caster's hands are too small to use the thumb alone, grasp the rod in front of the reel with the last three fingers and guide the line with the thumb and forefinger, working back and forth in front of the reel.

Practically all the higher grade reels have spiral gearing. That is, the gears are cut spirally on the pinion and driving gear, which causes two teeth of the latter to be always enmeshed with two in the pinion. This construction eliminates lost motion and produces a smoothness rivalling that of a belt-drive. Spiral gears, however, are just a refinement or added nicety, and it will be a long time before the common, simple, spur-tooth gearing is discontinued entirely.

Naturally the quality of the material used on the working parts of a reel have much to do with its price and its lasting and casting qualities. Pinions are usually of the highest grade of tool steel, gear journals are tempered, ground, lapped, and highly polished, and the driving gear is cut from solid bars of the best brass. Comparing the "works" of a high grade and a cheap reel through a magnifying glass tells a big story.

Most casting reels are equipped with click and drag. The click usually consists of a pawl and ratchet and is controlled by a thumb button. Its principal use is to keep the line from running out when the rod is not used in casting—as for example when carrying it to and from the boat. It also enables one to use his multiplying reel for fly-casting, although the common click reels with protected handle are best for this purpose. If strong enough it is also used in trolling as it does away with the necessity of continually keeping the thumb on the spool and it acts as an "alarm" when the line runs out. Most clicks, if used often, become weakened in time and the drag, which is a stronger brake, is then necessary. The drag has no value from a casting standpoint. Some beginners cast with the click "on" instead of learning to thumb the spool—this is "bad medicine" for the reel.

Both click and drag are controlled by thumb buttons in head of tail plate, or by a milled wheel in the rim of head and tail box. Just where these are located is a matter of small moment to the average caster.

Some reels are jeweled by having a piece of agate, garnet, or sapphire set in the center of the oil cap. The end of the pivot or end thrust runs on this and it no doubt reduces friction. This is called "cap jeweling." Hole jewels are jewels set in the pivot bushing and take the wear the whole length of the pivot. In the higher grade reels, cap jewels cost about $4 extra and we consider it a good investment, while the cap and hole jewels cost $10. We doubt if any but the most expert tournament casters have any need of jeweling of this kind. Incidentally, one of the makers of high grade reels has discontinued furnishing hole jeweling because he considers it unsatisfactory.

The oil caps of some reels are made 'compensating." That is, when the reel becomes worn the cap can be tightened slightly to take up lost motion, and this no doubt is a valuable feature in the lower priced reels.

The frame, spool, and end plates of a reel are either of nickel plated brass, hard rubber and brass, hard rubber and German silver, German silver, or, rarely, German silver and aluminum. Of course the brass and brass and rubber are used in the cheaper grades and they are the least desirable materials, although not so abominably bad as some writers paint them.

The rubber and silver construction makes a nice "contrasty" looking reel, and is plenty strong enough if the rubber is protected by metal bands. Otherwise it is liable to breakage, which is something to be avoided in a reel.

All the higher grade reels are made of German silver, sometimes with aluminum spools, and it is an ideal material for the purpose. It is strong, not too heavy, and while it tarnishes (which is a virtue up to a certain point) it can easily be "shined up."

High grade reels are not simply a matter of good materials, but of the very finest mechanical adjustment, and this adjustment had better not be disturbed by taking the reel apart, unless absolutely necessary— and then it had better be done by an expert.

The quadruple multiplying reel is purely an American invention, and not of so recent origin as some anglers seem to believe. The inventor to whom we owe the multiplier was probably George Snyder, of Paris, Ky., who made his first reel in 1810. Since that time, "Kentucky" reels have been famous the world over.

A few years ago, while fishing the rapids of the Maumee, in Ohio, we ran across a fisherman using one of these early Kentucky reels, which he assured us was made in 1849. It was in fairly good condition, quite free running, and although made of brass and having a crank instead of a balanced handle, it did not differ so very much from the modern article. The owner's grandfather and father had used it before him, and he told us that his son was then learning to cast. In fact, from what he said, we gathered that he was quite proficient in casting hints for that particular reel, which, by the way, should be retired "for distinguished services."

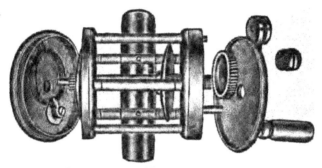

BLUEGRASS KENTUCKY REEL

As we held this four-generation reel in our hands, it brought visions of the days in which it was made— of prairie schooners and red-shirted miners. Just think of all the valiant bass, pickerel, pike, and even "muskies" (they were plentiful in the Ohio and its tributaries years ago) that this forty-niner has prospected for and found!

SIZES AND STYLES

In speaking of the sizes of reels, we usually say 80 yard, 100 yard, etc., but this is somewhat misleading as there is no particular size of line used as a standard. The measurements of the spool and pillars also vary in different makes, so that these must be specified if you have your heart set on a certain size. Generally an 80 yard reel of good proportions has a spool diameter of about 1½ inches, and pillars 1⅝ inches in length. Most experienced casters prefer the "long-spool" models, rather than the narrower, high end-plate type, as they permit easier spooling of the line and they are easier to thumb, the decrease in the size of the spooled line being more gradual.

For practical fishing purposes, the 80 and 100 yard sizes are generally used as they may also be utilized for trolling. A reel to balance a very light rod can be of the 60 yard size, as this size takes a 50 yard spool of line with plenty of allowance for swelling and does away with the necessity of fillers and arbors.

In casting the full capacity of the reel is seldom used, so it is customary to use a filler of old line or cheap linen line on the reel and to this tie on 50 yards or so of the casting line. This system not only economizes on line, but it fills up the spool so it is easier to thumb and increases the weight of the spool so that it casts easier. Also it keeps the line farther from the axis of the reel, which prevents any tendency of the line to foul on rod or guides.

The only objection to using a filler is the nuisance of drying it. It is bad enough, all casters agree, to have to dry the fishing line, much less bothering with from 20 to 50 yards of "padding." One remedy is to use an arbor, or drum of cork. By paying $1.00 extra, the reel-makers will furnish a cork arbor on their tournament grade reels, or one can be made by fitting pieces of cork on the spindle of the reel as described in Perry Frazer's book, "Fishing Tackle."

A simpler method which we have found very satisfactory, is as follows:

On the bare spindle of the reel, attach the line to be used, reel it up and tie on the end some old line. Reel on the old line until the spool is filled, making allowance for swell. Now pull off both lines and reverse, or put the old line on first. When this is all wound on tightly and evenly, cut off the end line, this being done to ascertain how much of the old line is to be used as the filler.

Then take one inch adhesive tape and wrap tightly around the old line. Three strips, one on each end and one in the middle, the latter over-lapping, will be about right. Now give the adhesive tape three coats of shellac and when dried, you have a good, hard water-proof arbor. The casting line, of course, is tied to this arbor. The advantage of this style is the fact that it can be removed with a sharp knife if one wants to troll or use more line than ordinarily, and that it can be put on without taking a reel apart.

Still another method we have heard of but never tried is to use common wrapping twine for a filler and to soak it in melted paraffine. This, of course, can only be done by removing the spool from the reel.

Practically all reels nowadays are made with balanced handle, rather than a common crank, the idea being that they run more smoothly. The position of the handle may be specified on the higher grade reels. Usually the handle is placed "forward of the bottom." That is directly under or ahead of the oil caps, near the bottom of the reel. This, it seems, is the logical place for the handle.

GRADES AND PRICES

Just what grade of reel to buy is the problem we will now attempt to "wrestle" with. Very often the beginner is "scared stiff" by the reckless statements made by some writers on angling topics to the effect that the reel worth casting with is an impossibility under $8 or $10. Quadruple multiplying reels range in price from 75 cents to $60. What grade to buy should depend on the angler's pocket-book and the amount of use the reel will get, the latter being more important.

For the once-in-a-while fisherman, a high grade reel would be an extravagance—something from $2.50 to $5.00 will be plenty good enough until he gets thoroughly inoculated with the fever. As is to be expected, such a reel will be of fairly soft material, not designed for long years of very hard service, but it will be a casting reel in every sense of the word. We have a reel which cost $4.50, that has seen seven years of hard service, and apparently it is good for several more years, and, incidentally, one of the best known practical casters in this country prefers a reel of a well-known make that sells for $5.00. Reels of this class make good "second" or emergency reels for the more persistent casters.

The next class to consider comprises the "week-enders," who outnumber all other types of fishermen ten to one. By week-enders, we mean fishermen living in city, town, or country, who leave home Friday night or Saturday noon, and return in time to be "back-on-the-job" Monday morning. Considering his numbers and the fact that he practically supports the tackle business, reel makers have given the week-ender and his needs more than passing attention. This kind of fisherman needs a good reel—the substantial middle class one that "will stand the gaff." While he does not fish often he fishes hard. Like the man who spent a week in Washington one Sunday morning, he does a week's fishing in a day or two.

This kind of caster, we would say, should pay something between $5 and $16—perhaps $20 should be his outside limit. There are some very good reels in this class as any experienced caster will testify, if he will just call them to mind.

The expert tournament caster and the skilled fisherman of means will perhaps satisfy a determination to have nothing but the very best and buy something at from $26 to $35, and such a reel, if given reasonably good care, will still be in good condition long after the man who buys it has creeled his last fish.

In buying a reel keep this fact in mind: it pays big dividends to buy one just a little better than you think you can afford.

SPECIAL FEATURE REELS

FREE SPOOL REELS

The free spool reel is one whose handle remains motionless while the cast is being made or when the line is running out. Years ago the gears were disengaged by turning a little lever or button and it surely was amusing to watch some absent-minded fisherman, who had forgotten to press the lever, vigorously turning the handle while a hooked fish was just as vigorously running away with the line. Later on these reels were made so that the gears would re-engage by pressing in on the handle. Now it is all done automatically —you simply turn the handle.

There is no doubt that free spool reels are very free running as there is little inertia and no air resistance of the handle to overcome. In fact most casters find that the free spool reel starts too suddenly until they become accustomed to using one. The free spool mechanism is contained in the head box of the reel and the caster owning a reel of this kind, if it can be taken apart easily, should carry an extra mechanism for emergencies although they are quite dependable.

SELF-THUMBING REELS.

The self-thumbing reels are those that have a check by mechanical means which prevents the reel over-running and thus eliminates backlashing. The old hand naturally can see no virtue in a self-thumbing reel.

It is, he says, too much like a self-aiming rifle and removes the element of skill.   On the other hand, one might say that instead of being like a self-aiming rifle it is like a telescope sight—making for more efficiency.

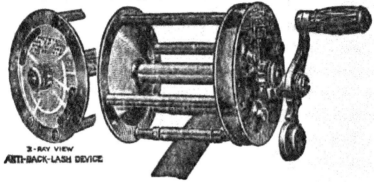

ENTERPRISE ANTI-BACK LASH REEL

There are at this writing only two makes of self-thumbers on the market.   The South Bend Anti Back Lash has a wire bail or brake that is held up and off by the outgoing line.   As the line loses momentum the bail gradually drops and applies the brake.   When the line stops the bail falls—the brake is on.   A thumb screw regulates the tension of the brake so that the reel can be adjusted for baits of different weight.

SOUTH BEND ANTI-BACK LASH REEL

The Redifor operates on an entirely different principle. It has small discs in the end plate of the reel that expand by centrifugal force when the spool is in motion and act as a brake or check. Both reels can be used as ordinary reels if desired; they are of German silver with jeweled caps and are well-made. Reels of this type are recommended only for the man who has neither the time nor inclination to learn to thumb the spool properly, which is not much of a job, by the way. They are well worth their cost as an arouser of enthusiasm in the Lady-Who-Lets-You-Go-Fishing. They are also handy for night casting.

Open Spool Reels

A comparatively recent development in reel construction is the open spool models. These are simply solid frame reels without the customary back and front pillars.

The advantages of this construction are the ease of spooling and the consequent reduction of backlashes; also the ease with which a backlash can be untangled. The absence of the pillars also permits the thumbing of the smooth flange of the spool instead of the line. Those who have trouble with "burned" thumbs from thumbing the line may find relief in an open spool reel although thumbing the flange is practiced by many casters with ordinary reels.

Level Winding Reels

Level winding reels are equipped with a mechanism

that automatically moves back and forth, as the handle is turned, the same as a caster's thumb, and lays the line on the spool evenly. In late years the mechanical excellence of these reels has been greatly improved, and they are now quite efficient and the prices are gradually being reduced.

One of the principal causes of backlashes is unevenly spooled lines and the level winding reels reduce this trouble to a minimum. The man who casts left-handed will find one of these reels a decided advantage, as it eliminates the shifting of the rod to the other hand preliminary to reeling in. The left-hander with a level winding reel can make five casts to the ordinary caster's four. These reels are also desirable for casting very early or very late in the season when the water is cold.

There are winding devices made to attach to ordinary reels that act as level winders. Personally, we have never used one but they seem to perform satisfactorily.

The "Beetzell" reel combines the self-thumbing, open spool, free spool, level winding features, the latter being particularly clever. It is not engaged while the line is running out but picks it up when the reeling in begins.

TAKE DOWN REELS

For a number of years manufacturers have been working to produce reels that can be easily taken apart without tools and without requiring any careful readjustment. There is no denying that this feature is highly desirable and the lack of it is the only objection anyone can find to the higher grade reels. Manufacturers of these tell us to send the reel back to the factory rather than attempt to take it apart ourselves and this is the nuisance. Of course you can take one of these reels apart but it must be reassembled very carefully. In fishing very sandy territory, like the dune country of Indiana and Michigan for example, a reel that cannot be taken apart frequently spoils many an otherwise good day.

Most Shakespeare reels are take down. By simply removing the spool caps and unscrewing two knurled pillars the reel comes apart in three pieces—the head

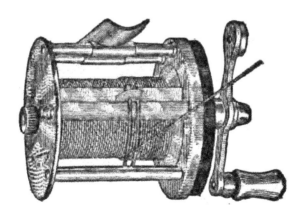

SHAKESPEARE REEL

plate with crank and gear and drag, the tail plate with click spring and pawl and the spool with pinion and click ratchet.

The Meisselbach Tak-A-Part and Tri-Part reels are take down. You simply unscrew a band on head and tail piece. The Meek, numbers 33 and 25, work on a similar principle, and other makers are giving considerable attention to the idea. Personally, we believe that at least one reel in the caster's outfit should be of the take down style.

CARE OF THE REEL

Reels are made nearly "fool proof." The only care required is a drop of oil on each end bearing after using and occasionally a drop in the crank. When you remove the handle to oil here be sure that it is screwed back tightly. By a drop of oil a drop of oil is meant. Too much oil slows up a reel and causes trouble. A "one drop oil can" is an important part of a bait caster's outfit. Oiling should be done every time the reel is used but an occasional cleaning is all that is required. The amount of use the reel gets should determine this.

Some reels are held together by only a few screws and this kind is more easily adjusted. Those with a screw in each pillar should be adjusted very carefully. Screws should be tightened just a trifle, each screw getting a slight turn alternately. Before loosening any screws test the spool for end play and time its running ability with the second hand of your watch and put it together again with the same amount of play— it should run a few seconds longer after it is cleaned.

Set the drag before taking the reel apart. When it is apart wash it in benzine. Clean the pivot and gear holes with a piece of chamois or a rag on a small hardwood stick. After cleaning put ONE drop of oil in each pivot hole, on the stud where the gears fit, and in the groove in the rear. Then grease the gears very lightly with vaseline or mutton tallow.

For taking a reel apart a screw-driver known as a "jeweler's model" is best. The blade revolves while the handle remains stationary so that it is unnecessary to remove the hand with every turn—price twenty-five cents.

Dust and sand are the reel's arch enemies and for protection against them the reel should be carried in a chamois bag or in a leather box made for the purpose. The bag costs about twenty five cents and the box about a dollar.

CHAPTER V

THE LINE.

NEXT to the reel the line is the most important part of the bait caster's equipment. It requires more, and gets less, attention than any part of the outfit. Silk is, so far, the only material suitable for casting lines. For years manufacturers have tried to find a substitute. Linen of various kinds has been tried as well as cotton and other materials, but they are unsuitable to begin with or soon develop some defect.

But to go to the tackle store and to simply ask for a silk line is not enough, because there are a great many kinds of silk lines. There are the oiled silk, and several different varieties of enameled lines, for instance, used in fly casting. Braided silk is the only line suitable for bait casting. But to complicate matters there are also several different kinds of braided silk lines. There is soft braid, hard braid, round braid, square braid, cored lines, and water-proof lines. There is also the question of size or strength. From this layout the beginner is expected to pick something suitable —and he has a man-size job on his hands.

In choosing a casting line we again bump into the eat-your-cake-and-have-it bugaboo that dogs our steps all through life. Casting efficiency and durability are the opposing considerations here as in rods. There is no doubt that the soft braided line is the best from the purely casting standpoint, but it has its limitations. Its chief fault is that it doesn't wear well, and if it does it becomes flimsy with a disagreeable tendency to stick to the reel or cling to the rod. Also, if it becomes wet, it absorbs water and swells on the reel and be-spatters you with every cast; it is disagreeable to use when the water is cold.

The hard braided line wears better but it casts harder. That is, it does not flow as smoothly from the reel and some casters claim it burns the thumb be-cause of its hardness.

Round braided lines are smoother and better look-ing than the square, but the square is more elastic and is therefore less likely to snap under a heavy and abrupt strain, and a fish cannot tear out a hook as easily because the elastic line acts as a spring between fish and reel.

Waterproof lines are ordinary lines treated by some process that renders them proof against absorption. They are strong but often develop a stickiness that prevents good casting and is not pleasant to the touch. This is more noticeable when the sun is hot. Water-proof lines are often useful when fishing with surface lures as a watersoaked line tends to pull down the head of a floating bait.

Probably the strongest lines are those braided over a silk core. Naturally they are not suitable for the finest casting but are employed usually for casting for very heavy fish, such as large pike and muskellunge.

Sizes of lines are designated by both letter and number, but some makers have complicated matters by using systems of their own. The surest way to get what you want is to specify the pounds test. As a rule, a number six line will test from ten to fourteen pounds; number five from twelve to sixteen pounds; number four from sixteen to twenty-two pounds depending on the style and make. These three sizes are all the caster will ever have much use for. Sizes that are lettered usually start with C for Number One; D, Number Two; E, Number Three; and so on down to size Six or H.

Braided silk lines are tested dry by dead weight and not by pulling against spring balances or scales. A bag of shot is frequently used. The mere fact that one can break a line with the hands does not mean that it will not "hold" a big fish. We have taken large bass and pickerel on a line testing seven pounds, but some margin of safety is desirable due to the fact that silk lines deteriorate. The best all-round line is one testing 14 or 16 pounds.

Color is a matter or debate among casters. Some swear by white lines, others are equally positive that nothing can equal one of black or green or ticked black and white. Personally, we don't believe that color makes a great deal of difference to the fish, but we have a suspicion that dyeing does not help a line any. Possibly there is something in the theory of using a green line in the weeds and a light colored one in the clear waters of some spring-fed lakes. A conservative middleground sort of line is the mottled black and white or salt and pepper which becomes nearly gray or neutral when wet—you will find more good lines of this color than any other.

There is an intimate relationship between the rod and line, and what we have said of the short rods and heavy fishing and long rods and open water fishing applies to the line as well. In other words when you are fishing open water and using a light rod and light lure nothing equals a soft braid line testing ten or twelve pounds or even less. For the more strenuous get-him-into-the-boat-quick style of fishing or when using heavy plugs a heavier hard braid line is more in keeping with the fitness of things.

As a general rule, casters expect too much of a line. They fail to consider that it is nothing but fine silk —animal matter. The principal causes of deterioration are friction in casting, sand, rust, alkali, and other chemicals in the water, mildew, and "sweat rot."

The friction of continual casting is terrific—friction usually shows by a "fuzziness" or a frayed appearance near the bait end or, in case of a square braid line, by its "running flat." Agate guides and tip-top help considerably in reducing friction. Naturally there is more friction when using a heavy bait.

Sand plays havoc with a silk line and should be avoided as much as possible. Rust is death to silk line, destroying it quickly wherever it comes in con-

tact with it. Avoid fastening lines to rusty nails
when drying them or placing the reel in a tackle box
that is rusted inside.

Nearly all waters are more or less alkaline which
sometimes has a chemical action on silk, especially
when the stream or lake is fed by mineral springs
containing iron salts. The action of alkalies and other
chemicals shows on colored lines by fading them quickly.

Mildew and sweat rot are caused by minute organisms in the water getting into the fiber of the line
and then decomposing. This decomposition generates
heat and soon spoils the silk.

When the caster fishes in water that deteriorates
his lines quickly he should use water-proof lines or at
any rate oil his line. Better still is the now popular
"dry line casting" which wets only the last few feet
of the line except of course when a fish is hooked and
played. In this style of fishing the rod is held a little
higher than usual and when a backlash occurs, the
untangled line is not stripped from the reel, permitting the line that is out to become water-soaked,
but it is taken into the boat and the snarl is then untangled. It is decidedly more pleasant to fish with
a dry line and it permits much nicer work. There
is really no necessity of wetting more than the last
two or three feet of line.

Different casters use different methods of line economy. Practically all dry their lines after using, as
this is necessary to prevent it rotting on the reel. Lines
should not be dried in the sun if it can be avoided;

the usual method is to stretch them between trees, or wrap them around the legs of chairs or some similar object. Some snip off from nine inches to a foot every hour or so when at "work"; others oil their lines to prevent absorption. Oiling is a good thing for a line, but there is no need of oiling it all—just that part that becomes wet.

To oil a line string it between two trees and rub it with a rag or piece of chamois skin saturated with a good light oil—reel oil is good enough—or melted tallow. Just before re-winding it on the reel take a soft dry rag and go over the line to remove surplus oil. After the line has dried is a good time to oil it.

Oiling is more or less bother, and an easier method is to use about fifteen feet of waterproof line on the business end of the cast. This gives the strength and weight where it is needed combined with the casting efficiency of the light soft braid line. The knot connecting the two lines must be very small and tight so as not to foul on the guides.

The practice of using a line-dryer is a good one, not only from the standpoint of convenience, but economy as well. When the line is on a drier, it can be washed in rain water removing mildew spores, algae, rust, sand, alkalies, and other chemicals. Silk lines may be used in salt water if thoroughly rinsed afterwards. A handy man can make a suitable line-drier, although they are now being marketed that fasten to the rod handle, and the line is reeled on to it directly from the reel and then back again when dried without removing the reel from the rod. They are collapsible and easily carried in the tackle-box. They cost two dollars and will save this much in lines in a season or two.

How long a line should last depends on the guides, the weight of baits used, the amount of casting done, the water, and the care the line gets. Offhand, we would say that no line, except the heavy, very hard braided line, is good for more than thirty hours casting, and few last that long under average conditions. With light, soft braid lines, many expert casters will use one end one day, dry it, and put the used end of the line on the reel first the next time, use it a day, and then throw it away. It is a safe method, no doubt, but some casters would consider from thirty-five cents to a dollar every day for line an extravagance.

The caster should not use the braided silk line for trolling or still-fishing, as with these methods it becomes thoroughly soaked and is likely to deteriorate rapidly. Have a separate line for this work. Enameled line is by far the best for this purpose.

To say how much or how little one should pay for a line is a good way to start an argument. By its very nature silk line, regardless of quality, will not last very long, so we believe it is better to get medium-priced lines, and get them oftener, than to depend solely upon high quality. A dollar for a fifty yard spool is enough to pay for ordinary fishing, and for seventy-five cents fifty yards of perfectly good line may be had.

Fifty yards is enough to put on the reel at one time —to fill the reel put on a filler of old line or a ten cent No. 6 linen one, or better still, use an arbor as mentioned in the chapter on reels. Before putting a new line on the reel, always take the kinks out. The best way to do this is to drag it, just as it comes from the spool with no weight on the end, through the grass. Next best, drag it through the water behind the boat, also with no weight.

The best way to carry braided silk lines over the winter is to wash them in rainwater, dry carefully in the shade, and put in a fruit jar with the lid tightly fastened.

Summary

For best casting: soft square braid line, small diameter, testing not more than twelve pounds. Durability poor; absorption greatest.

For durability: hard round braid line, testing about sixteen pounds. Casting quality fair; absorption less.

For alkaline or other deteriorating waters: waterproof line. Casting quality fair; absorption least.

For heaviest fishing: cored line, testing from eighteen to twenty-four pounds. Casting quality poorest.

To prevent deterioration: test line often while fishing and remove what breaks off easily. Either oil last few feet of line or tie to end a few feet of heavier waterproof line. Wash line in rainwater whenever possible, and dry in shade or on drier before putting away.

CHAPTER VI

MISCELLANEOUS TACKLE

THE bait caster's outfit should be simple. Rod, tackle box, and the means of landing a fish, reel, line, a few baits, odds and ends in the which can be either a net or gaff, are ample. Probably the most sportsmanlike method of landing a fish is with the bare hands, by sinking thumb and forefinger in the eye sockets of fish with teeth, and by grabbing a bass by the under jaw, which prevents him shaking. Sportsmanship must sometimes give way to efficiency, however, which calls for something more certain.

The landing net is an old and tried institution we inherited from our trout-fishing ancestors. To be of real help to the bait caster a landing net for boat use must be of good size—frame at least 16 inches in diameter, and with a strong, deep net. For the sake of convenience, most net-frames are made collapsible, so they can be easily carried or packed in a rod-case or suit case.

In buying one be sure it is not the kind that will collapse when a whopping big fish starts fighting for life, liberty, and the pursuit of happiness in it. Handles are usually of two pieces, jointed—see that the ferrule

TYPES OF CASTING "PLUGS"

Left to right: 1. Coaxer surface bait—single hooks; 2. Yellow Kid surface bait—revolving head type; 3. Baby Crab semi-surface bait—note upturned double hooks; 4. The original "Wabbler."—Wilson fluted; 5. Bassorew semi-surface bait—note single detachable hooks; 6. Bucktail minnow underwater bait—note swivelled snap-sinker for added weight; 7. Angular bodied Dowagiac—underwater bait.

SOME FAVORITE LURES

Left to right: 1. Tandem spinner weedless—Red Ibis Fly and pork strip—note dipsey swivelled sinker for added weight; 2. Frog on a weedless hook—frog is straddling main hook; 3. A pair of shiners on a Delavan spoon; 4. Pork chunk on a weedless hook—considered an artist's lure.

A STUDY IN SPINNERS

Left to right: 1. Fluted spoon with a feathered treble; 2. Willow leaf or close spinning spinner with Parmachene Belle fly; 3. Idaho or wide spinning spinner with Professor fly; 4. Standard or medium spinning spinner with Bucktail fly; 5. Pearl spinner with Grizzly King fly; 6. Weedless hook with spinners on weed guards.

is strong. The wooden handles are heavier than the bamboo and the latter is preferable. The four foot handle is a handy size for boat work, and a net so equipped can also be used on the stream by leaving one joint at home.

Landing net frames without net, as they are usually sold, cost from $1 to $3.

In nets we have a variety to choose from. The standard linen net, of ¾-inch mesh in the 24-inch size, costs about 25 cents; the brown waterproof 50 cents, while the waterproof, braided linen, which is the best, comes at $1.00. For use when fishing with single hooks, the net is to be preferred, but with the multi-hooked plugs, it is a nuisance. The hooks that are not in the fish, have a habit of catching on the net frame, which gives Mr. Fish just the leverage he wants to tear the hooks free, and if they don't catch on the frame, rest assured they will in the net. Untangling hooks from a landing net is bad for the net and the fisherman's temper.

When using an artificial bait with more than one hook, some form of gaff is better. The little jointed gaff with three 7 inch joints, is handy, but is made of brass tubing, and is not overly strong. They should be made with long steel joints like a Winchester or Marble rifle cleaning rod.

A satisfactory landing device is a clincher gaff. This is only 18 inches long, packs into a suit case, does not mutilate the fish and it holds. You simply place it over the fish and clench your hand. It will hold a fish up to 20 pounds, providing, of course, it has been played sufficiently.   It costs $1.00.

For very large fish, a large sharp gaff hook is needed, and sometimes it is advisable to shoot the fish with a pistol or revolver before taking him into the boat.   Of course, you can use the Gloucester fisherman's method of landing a large fish.   That is, by tipping the boat and permitting the fish to float in, but this is not recommended for the average man.

Beware of the hook without handle, which the tackle catalogue says "Can be cut from any tree."   You go fishing to fish, not to prowl around the woods looking for a gaff handle which you probably won't find.

Swivels are not used as much by casters as by trollers, but a few should be carried.   Let them be brass barrel swivels, sizes 4, 5, and 6, which cost about a penny each.   Strange but true, you still find fishermen using the split ring.   Better, in fact almost indispensable, to the caster, is the snap swivel, or swivel snap.   Tied on the end of the line it affords quick means of changing baits and will hold about anything that swims in fresh water.   Those with Number 4 swivels are about right.   They cost about 50 cents a dozen.

Gut leaders are of no use to the caster, but the wire traces are.   They prevent pike or pickerel biting the line.   Those of piano wire are stiff and interfere with the action of some baits, especially wobblers.   Better still is the flexible wire leader.   It is made of picture cord, with a loop or barrel swivel at one end and a swivel snap at the other. By all means get a few of these. They are usually 6 to 8 inches long, and cost about 15 cents each. The heavy jointed wire traces are good for very large fish.

Plain hooks are used only occasionally by bait casters, and then with natural bait. Either the hand forged O'Shaughnessy, the sproat, the Model Perfect, or the Cincinnati bass, will be found satisfactory. Special hooks will be discussed in the proper place.

A few plain ringed or Rangely sinkers should be carried by the caster for still fishing, but the caster's favorite sinker is the swiveled dipsey, used as extra casting weight with spinners and other light lures. Numbers 7, 8, and 9, weighing $\frac{1}{8}$, $\frac{1}{4}$, and $\frac{3}{8}$ ounces respectively and costing about 35 cents a dozen, are the most useful. Of particular usefulness is the snap swivel sinker, which is simply an ordinary cigar-shaped sinker with a swivel snap at one end—just the thing for added weight to small bodied plugs. Another useful sinker with a swivel snap at one end—just the thing for adding weight for live bait and to make it ride right side up in the water. These types of sinkers weigh about a quarter of an ounce and cost 10 cents each.

Stringing the fish through the gills and dragging them all over the lake is hard on the fish and frequently drowns them. It is better to kill the fish immediately and then string them. The stringer with little hooks that go through the fish's lips and leave the gills untouched is an improvement in stringers. A stringer with a sharp stringing needle is useful as the needle can be run up through the fish's chin and out through the nostril which keeps the fish's mouth closed and prevents drowning. When the fish do not run large, the fish bag is a good idea. This is a net bag with an elastic puckering string cleverly kept closed by a number of little brass rings. The frame of the opening is hollow, and contains enough air space to float all the fish the bag will hold. With it you can never lose your string of fish by tying it insecurely.

The Tackle Box and Its Contents

The stay-at-home, or stock tackle box, can be of any size desired—the bigger the better—and can be of any material, but the box you carry with you should be "smallish." The leather boxes are good as they stand lots of banging around, but they are expensive. The galvanized boxes are strong, but heavy. For inexpensiveness and general utility the tin boxes seem to meet all requirements. We have one that measures 4 x 5 x 11 and cost something like 65 cents, and for short trips when we carry a suit case, we have never felt the need of a larger or more elaborate one. As an extra precaution, however, with these tin boxes, it is a good idea to run a line of solder around the seams on the inside, to keep the water out, and to touch up all the bare spots with a little enamel now and then —the same enamel you use to cover worn spots on the steel rod.

Personally, we do not like narrow high boxes, as they are top-heavy; besides the box should be constructed so all the contents are "get-at-able" at once. For this reason the trayless suit case type of box is handy.

For either long trips where considerable tackle is taken, or for the one day trips, when the suit case is left at home, we use the metal "kit-bag" which is made along the lines of a traveling bag. It carries plenty of tackle, and in addition there is room for the rubber shirt, lunch, and other odds and ends.

Our small box, which we carry in the suit case, has one tray with five divisions, and to give the uninitiated some idea as to proper equipment, we are going to permit you to look through it.

In one tray is a small tin tobacco box containing an assortment of plain ringed hooks; a few swivels and swivel snaps occupy another. The larger compartment holds a few eyed flies and spinners for immediate use, the main stock of flies being in a 50-cent eyed fly box and spinners in a two-pocket card case, such as is given away by banks for advertising purposes. The next contains a few weedless pork hooks, some dipsey swivel sinkers, a few swivel snap sinkers, and "belly-down" weights. The fifth holds a hank of red darning cotton and a few small pieces of red flannel for pork rind.

The eyed fly box, the spinner book, extra lines, a small pair of pliers, scales, and a few favorite casting plugs go in the main compartment below the tray. In the reel compartment we carry either a cheap double multiplying reel "loaded" with linen line for trolling and still fishing, or an emergency casting reel, filled with silk line, depending on circumstances. In the long narrow division in the back of the box, we carry a few weedless pork and frog tandems, a minnow harness, leaders or traces, folding metal ruler, screw driver, small file, one drop oil can, and a dozen snelled hooks on a metal hook carrier. Artificial baits we carry in waterproof pocket books, one plug to a pocket. The reels are in boxes and are wrapped in the flannel shirt and go in the suit case along with the gaff or net.

Of course, we realize that this is only half of what some casters carry, and a great deal more than is necessary for an ordinary trip, but with this outfit we are prepared for any bass, pike, or pickerel waters; with the addition of a few large hooks, large spoons and a bucktail or so we are also equipped for muskellunge.

We do not offer this as model equipment by any means, but we could use this outfit in any fresh water on the continent, excepting trout streams, of course, without embarrassment or trouble through lack of tackle and we could, and very often do, help out some improvident brother of the craft. To save time and space, we will not tell of the things we once carried and discarded.

CHAPTER VII

ARTIFICIAL AND NATURAL BAITS

BAIT casting received its first great impetus toward popularity with the advent of the short rod, and the artificial bait, by which we mean the wooden or metal casting plug.

Without attempting to draw any odious comparisons, artificial baits possess certain advantages over live or natural bait that bulk large in the eyes of the average angler. In the first place, live bait is not always obtainable, you must know where to find it, then you must catch or dig it, and, finally, you must give it more or less care to keep it in usable condition. All this is troublesome and fishermen who count each moment golden are not likely to grow enthusiastic over anything that takes unnecessary time and labor.

Aside from its great convenience, however, your true and confirmed plug caster believes (and in a great many instances is ready to fight for his beliefs) that taking all conditions of water and weather into consideration, the artificial will catch more fish and bigger fish than will live bait. Also, the impaling of a live minnow, worm, or struggling frog on a hook is decidedly distasteful to some people.

On the other hand, some fishermen object to the artificial, claiming that it is unsportsmanlike, that owing to its weight it does not give the fish a fair fighting chance, and that one might as well use a net as the gangs of treble hooks that grace (or disgrace, depending on your viewpoint), the average casting plug. Also they say that the treble hooks frequently snag fish and that this fact makes the plug inhumane. The fact that some of our most expert casters take this stand on casting plugs gives weight to these contentions.

Whatever the facts may be, it is interesting to note that both sides of the controversy raise the question of humaneness, which shows that their hearts are in the right place, even if their reasoning powers are not. Personally we believe that there is truth in both sides of the question.

We believe further that the questionable sportsmanship or ethics of the artificial will eventually be adjusted. Some states, New Jersey and Michigan, for example, have passed laws limiting the number of hooks to a bait, or putting a limit on the bait's size, and the tendency with each passing year is toward smaller, lighter lures and fewer hooks. Besides there is nothing to prevent the conscientious fisherman replacing treble hooks with single or double ones.

That treble hooks are unmitigated nuisances is beyond doubt. They tangle themselves up when two or more baits are carried together, and they have a habit of catching on weeds, logs, and other snags while in the water, and at other times on the landing net, clothing, and not infrequently human flesh, in a way that is disconcerting to say the least. But they are highly efficient as to hooking ability, and since most fishermen go fishing to catch fish, we doubt if the treble hook will ever be eliminated entirely unless by legislation.

Most makers of casting plugs will supply their baits with single or double hooks at no extra expense, and some makers have been studying for years to produce a substitute for treble hooks. At least one manufacturer equips his baits with double belly-hooks that point inwards and upwards, and the bait being round rolls when struck, thus presenting at least one barb to the fish. Another has produced what is called the "Dummy Double" hook. It is really a single hook, with an extra bend to give leverage for "setting" the actual hook. Neither of these hooks quite equals the treble in hooking efficiency, but both are superior to it as regards snagging and tangling. Thus you see our old friend Nemesis (the necessity of sacrificing one advantage to gain another) is still on our trail.

Still another maker turns out plugs with a detachable single hook that may be snapped on or off at will. The hook is well made and we have found it quite the equal of the treble in hooking qualities.

Anglers disagree as to how bass, pike, and muskellunge strike an artificial bait, but as a general rule bass strike from the side, seizing the bait in the jaw and not in the gullet. Pickerel usually strike from the rear, while the muskellunge most often from the side and upwards.

We once brought up the question of how a fish hits a bait with a grizzled old guide, and he agreed that they generally strike as stated above. However, he added: "Sometimes they sees it an' hits it an' that's all there is to it," which was his way of expressing a truism laid down by Samuel Camp that "a fish usually knows that the shortest distance between two points is a straight line."

We quoted this to old Pete in our discussion and he came back with this: "An' that's a helofa sight more'n some folks knows."

The way a fish strikes a bait, has considerable bearing on hook placement, and the position of the hooks on a bait is of more importance than the number or style of hooks. The hooks must be placed with a "killing angle"; that is, so attached that they present at least one barb to the fish that strikes no matter how he does it.

Since a fish must necessarily strike a surface bait from below, most "floaters" are made with belly-gangs or hooks attached to the bottom of the bait.

Underwater plugs usually have hooks attached to or suspended from the sides. Sometimes they have as many as two gangs of trebles on each side, which, together with a tail gang, makes 15 barbs, which is obviously overdoing a good thing.

Those with two side gangs at the very most, and a tail gang, hook just as many strikes and in our experience get more strikes because of their smaller size, than do the super-dread-naught type. Nine hooks is all we would recommend, and we have learned that one belly-gang will do the work of two side-gangs.

With underwater baits with two belly-gangs, you can usually remove the tail hooks without danger of losing any fish. In short, regardless of the ethics of the case the better the placement of the hooks, the fewer hooks that are necessary, and the consequent fewer snags and other inconveniences of multi-hooked plugs.

In studying the placement of hook, the bait should be held in the hand with the head pointing almost straight up, which will put the hooks in about the position they will be when the bait is traveling in the water.

In weight, casting plugs run from a quarter of an ounce to nearly a full ounce. The smaller plugs are usually the most effective and, of course, when the heavier ones are used, it requires a sturdy rod and a heavy line.

Casting plugs range in price from 10 cents to $1.00 or more, with an average of about 60 or 75 cents. To the uninitiated, the only difference between the cheaper plug and the higher grades, is the price, but a well made plug is usually worth its cost. Cheap plugs are made of inferior wood, painted instead of enameled, the spinners are usually spinners in name only, the hooks are poor and stuck on with no regard to killing angle, and the whole contraption often goes to pieces at unexpected times—usually when you have hooked your biggest fish.

The products of reputable makers are always well made. The wood is flawless cedar, treated to prevent warping, the colors are permanent and the celluloid enamel, besides giving a desirable flashiness, will stand a lot of use and abuse, before chipping. The spinners spin, the hooks are strong and properly placed, the weight and size are so related that the bait rides in the water properly and the metal is heavily plated to guard against rust. Metal baits are not so easily imitated cheaply and most of them can be relied upon.

With a reasonable amount of care, a well-made plug will last several seasons. Slamming it against rocks or pilings is bound to put the hooks and spinners out of commission, and eventually to crack the enamel. Keep the hook points well filed, and beware of rust— it dulls the hooks, loses fish, and there is less danger of infection if you accidently get caught on a bright hook. Incidentally, if you should get hooked with the barb well in, heroic treatment is necessary—push the hook all the way through and then cut it off with a pair of pliers. Tincture of iodine is a good antiseptic and a small vial of it should be carried on trips into the wilderness.

Many theories have been advanced as to why a fish will attack an artificial bait. Some think it arouses the appetite of the fish, that the fish that strikes some time or other has eaten something of the same color. Others say that the fish's fighting or killing instinct is aroused. Most casters probably have noticed how the minnows scurry away from their plug when it is being retrieved, and the fish often see this too and attack the bait because it, obviously, is a marauder raiding the food supply.

A fish sees a bait in the air because most of them feed from the air as well as from the water, he hears the splash and sees the flash of the enamel and spinners, and he proceeds at once to the attack. Color has an influence on fish, too. The reason a fish will savagely attack one color one day and not look at it another is something that has never been explained and very probably never will be.

You know what happens when the fair summer boarder with a red parasol crosses the domain of the mean, horrid, old gentleman cow. Well, just that happens when a highly colored plug crosses the bailiwick of a testy-tempered fish!

We are told that the idea of the casting plug had its origin in this way: Once upon a time a fisherman was seated in his boat on a small Michigan lake, cussing his luck. He had worked hard and the rewards were small. He decided to quit for the day, and lighting his last cigarette, he hurled the gaudily colored box far out into the lake. It no sooner struck the water when it went sailing skyward. Not being of the comic newspaper type of angler, who carries his bait in a jug, he was more than surprised, and pinched himself to see if he was dreaming. No, there it went sailing skyward again. He investigated and found that a bass was venting his rage on the colored box, so securing it, he attached a couple of hooks, and soon had Mr. Bass on his string.

This tale may not be probable, but it is possible. We have seen fingerling bass make savage rushes at burned Swedish safety matches—the lavender colored ones—that smokers had thrown in the water, and almost every bass fisherman can call to mind similar observations.

Surface Baits or "Floaters"

Show a collection of surface baits, without their hooks, to a non-fisherman, and he would probably venture the guess that they represented the life work of some perpetual motion "expert" residing permanently at Mattewan, N. Y., Dunning, Ill., or some similar place. Surely most of them resemble nothing that flies in the air, walks or crawls on the earth, or swims in the waters beneath the earth.

The success of floating baits depends principally upon their ability to "muss-up" the surface of the water, and this end is achieved by means of exaggerated heads or metal collars in the non-mechanical types, or by revolving fronts, spinners, or propeller-like paddle wheels in the other kind.

Whether or not the commotion on the water made by these baits, imitates the struggles of some swimming "critter" as some claim, we cannot say, although the supposition is reasonable enough, but that it often induces fish to strike, we can and do state very emphatically.

The use of "floaters" is one of the most pleasurable forms of fishing. When you see an old he-bass dash 20 or 30 feet for a surface bait, and that bait is on the end of your line, the business end of the rod to which that line and lure are attached is no place for a nervous lady! The surface bait cannot be used, as some seem to believe, at all times and under all conditions—sometimes the fish will not rise to the surface.

Surface baits are at their best when the fish are in shallow water and usually this means early and late in the season, or after sundown in midsummer. The best hours are from daylight until ten o'clock in the morning, from four in the afternoon until dark, and from "moon-up" until midnight. On dull days with overcast skies, they can be used successfully all day.

As with all casting plugs, long distance casting is not ordinarily productive of fish, except when the water is very smooth and very clear. True, one is likely to get more strikes on long casts, but landing a fish with more than 100 feet of line out is always a very doubtful proposition.

Short casts and lots of them is the best system, as most strikes are produced the instant the bait "hits" the water or very soon thereafter—the short caster makes the most casts and usually gets the most fish. As the splash is an attraction, and because a fish who sees a bait in the air can move to meet it when it "lands" casting moderately high is usually most success-ful. High casts can be made by having considerable line between the head of the bait and the tip of the rod. Start the bait back quickly, before it hits the water in fact, because a bait that lies motionless even an instant, looks suspicious and the fish will hesitate to strike it.

The fish that hesitates is lost—to the fisherman. Reel fairly fast. If the fish are "striking short" slow up. At times vary your reeling, moving the bait alternately slowly and fast. As soon as you get a strike, set the hooks with a quick jerk upwards. Don't believe all you hear about fish hooking themselves on treble hooks.

With few exceptions, hooks on floating baits are placed on the belly rather than on the sides, and in a well designed plug the head of the bait rides high in the water. This creates more of a "riffle" on the surface and presents the hooks properly. Either a waterproof line or one well oiled toward the end, should be used by the beginner as a water-soaked line drags the head of the bait down unduly.

White body with red head seems to be the favorite color of most casters, with yellow body and black or bronze spots a close second. Next in order we would rank white body with blue head, solid yellow, solid white or luminous, frog colors, solid gray. We once heard an "old hand" cover the subject of surface bait colors as follows: "I don't care what color the plug is, just so the belly is white or yellow."

THE SEMI-SURFACE BAIT OR WOBBLER

The semi-surface bait is a comparatively new member of the casting plug family, but in its few years of existence it has gone far and has demonstrated beyond doubt its ability to catch fish. We believe it to be the deadliest of all casting plugs—it is a "meat-bait," rather than a sporting proposition. It possesses the advantages of all other types of artificials, such as size and showiness in the air, color and splash, in addition to a very strike-inducing "flight" while in the water.

It floats on the surface (which is a decided advantage to the beginner when he is untangling back-lashes) until reeled in. Then it dives and darts, or wobbles, from side to side and travels from a few inches to several feet deep, depending upon what kind of a wobbler it is and how fast it is retrieved. Unlike the under-water plug, the faster a wobbler is reeled, the deeper it goes.

The erratic motion of this type of bait is a good imitation of the movements of a crippled, or badly frightened minnow—the stray lamb which is the favorite prey of the wolves of the water.

There are two general types of wobblers—those that travel in fairly wide sweeps, the wobbler proper, and those with the deadly tail wobble which might be called the wriggler type. They seem to be equally effective, one being preferred one day, the other the next, with seemingly no well-defined rule for their use. The small bodied wobblers can be made to wriggle by re-moving the tail gang of hooks, and if the rear belly-gang is placed well back, the absence of the tail hooks does not affect the general hooking ability of the bait. Nearly all wobblers are made with belly-gangs which explodes the old theory that baits used beneath the surface must have side hooks.

Different makers of these baits use different methods of obtaining the desired wobble, such as flutings, angu-lar or concave heads, and metal wings. Some have wings of flexible metal and upper and lower line fast-enings (the screw eyes by which the bait is attached to the line), so that the angle of resistance is changed, making the bait travel at different depths as desired. This type of wobbler can also be used as a surface bait.

The original wobbler was red and white, and this is undoubtedly the most killing coloration under aver-age conditions. We would rank the other colors, in the order named, as follows: solid red (for clear water); solid yellow or yellow and red (for cloudy water); rainbow (especially for pickerel); green and white.

As to general usefulness, the wobblers are versatile. We have caught fish with them under practically every condition of water and weather that fish can be caught, which we realize is a pretty sweeping statement.

Ideal wobbler water is that where the tops of the weeds do not come quite to the surface. Nearly all lakes and some streams have beds of weed growth of this kind. The best way to fish under these conditions is to start on the windward side of the weeds, preferably keeping near the edge, and drift over, casting ahead of you as you go. Make short casts and lots of them. Keep the tip of the rod pointing at the bait and reel just fast enough to clear the tops of the weeds. When you come to an obstruction of any kind stop reeling and permit the bait to float over. Two men fishing in a boat over a weed bed of this kind can cover the water very thoroughly.

Other shallow places like bars, flats, and gravel beds near islands and points are also good places to try the wobbler. In small lakes and slow streams or where the weeds come to or above the surface, keep out fifty or sixty feet and cast in as near the weeds as possible without snagging. Don't overlook the "pockets" or indentations in the edge of the weed line, because that is where the big fellows are likely to be loafing. Because of its darting motion a wobbler when it catches on a weed does so in a way that makes your heart jump. Give a slight lift of the rod whenever you feel any resistance—it may be a fish!

Another place for the wobbler is where there is "patchy" bottom—alternate spots of sand and gravel and bottom moss or other small weed growth. This type of bottom is usually in shallow water. Sometimes it is a natural condition; more often it is an old spawning bed of bass or sunfish. Bass and pickerel both love to lie in the protection of the weeds and watch the clear spots, since minnows also choose places of this kind for their feeding and playground. If you know places with this kind of bottom by all means give your wobbler a trial even if the water is ridiculously shallow and no one in the memory of the oldest inhabitant has ever been known to catch fish there.

While the wobbler is used most effectively in water that is shallow or of moderate depth it can be used successfully in deep water at times. Make long casts down the wind and reel as fast as possible is the system to use then.

Underwater Baits or Wooden Minnows

The underwater plug is the original wooden or artificial "minnie." You will often find one or two of them in the tackle boxes of even confirmed live bait fishermen who use them for trolling.

As a casting bait the underwater type is not as popular as it used to be for several reasons. In the first place, the average caster prefers a bait that will float so that when he is untangling a back-lash it will not settle in the weeds and refuse to come up again, which is a calamity that costs on an average about sixty cents. Also it is over-shadowed at present by the wobbler which catches fish even in inexperienced hands. Nevertheless the underwater is beyond doubt a good bait when properly used.

The "old hand" catches fish with this bait because he knows how to handle it. He makes fairly long casts, reels slowly enough for the bait to travel deep, and manipulates his rod tip and reel handle so that the lure travels erratically, similar to the movements of the wobbler.

Underwater plugs are the most effective in fairly deep water—too deep for good results, ordinarily, with wobblers and surface baits. This means that you must reel slowly to get your bait down because the underwater is so weighted that it sinks deeper the slower you reel. The best way to use it is to reel, stop and let your bait sink a little, reel, stop and so on, with an occasional twitch of the rod tip first to one side, then to the other. This is awkward at first but is soon mastered. Of course when fishing in a stream full of snags the bait must be reeled fast enough to keep it away from the bottom. To fish very deep use a small bodied bait and hook to it a snap swivel sinker to keep its head down.

If your underwater plug gets snagged in the weeds, don't try to pull it loose by main strength. Row directly over it, then grasp the line as far down as possible and a few sharp tugs will usually free it.

Color seems to play a more important part in this class of bait than in floaters or wobblers and certain colors are apparently best in certain waters. For example, the rainbow coloration, green back, red uppers, yellow sides, cream belly, is usually the favorite on large, clear, spring fed bodies of water; the solid red in the marl bottomed lakes in Michigan and other states; the solid yellow or solid white in marshy, dark water lakes and streams; the green cracked back, white belly, on fast, clear streams for small mouth bass.

The theory is to use dark plugs on clear days and in clear water and light ones for dark days, but no hard and fast rules can be followed.

Most underwater baits are equipped with spinners which should be kept well greased with vaseline. When there are two spinners, one at each end as is usually the case, they are made to spin in opposite directions so as to not kink the lines, but it is safer to use a swivel snap, nevertheless.

Spoons, Spinners, and Flies

Various reasons are offered to account for the success of the spoon or spinners as a lure. Some experts say it is due to the irritating light rays it throws in the eyes of the fish; others that the fish looks upon the lure as an invader threatening his commissary, and still others claim that the fish mistakes it for a minnow or food of some kind. While these theories are interesting, the mere fact that spinners and spoons catch fish is of much more importance to most of us.

The first bait of this character, so far as is known, was used some time in the early part of the last century. It was simply the bowl of a common teaspoon with a hook soldered to the point or narrow end. A hole was bored in the upper end by which it was fastened to a straight piece of wire—very similar in principle, you will note, to what is used to-day. This original spoon caught fish, but with the years improvements were added and now the spoon or the spinner is a marvel of efficiency. Few fishermen realize the amount of study that has been devoted to this type of lure.

The first requisite of a spinner or spoon is that it spins freely and easily. This result can be obtained only by correct design of blade and its attachment to the shank. Spinning is often aided by beads of glass or metal which act as bearings. A valuable feature from the caster's standpoint, which is lacking in many trolling spoons, is a system of attaching the blade so that it swings back and travels, when cast, "belly up," so it offers little resistance to the air. This reversible, hinged lug construction is valuable when a fish is hooked, as the blade remains strictly neutral in the ensuing battle by not catching on the weeds and grass. An easy spinner does away with the necessity of using swivels, which is of value to the caster as every joint adds to the liability of tangling up while in the air.

The terms "spinner" and "spoon" are generally used to signify the same thing although strictly speaking the spoon is used mostly for trolling while the spinner is of lighter construction and is designed especially for casting.

Every conceivable shape or design is used in making spinners or spoons, but the approved patterns are the willow leaf, the kidney, and the standard spoon-shaped type.

The willow leaf is long and slender and spins very close to the shank and is a good imitation of a swimming minnow. It is most valuable in fairly clear waters. The kidney design or Idaho is somewhat rounded, spins out from the shank and is used mostly in "roily" water, while the standard shape is for normal conditions, all of this depending on the finish of the blades.

No complaint can be made as to the variety of finishes offered. While nearly all blades are made of brass they are finished by plating in nickel, brass, copper, silver, gold, white enamel, red enamel, and different combinations of these. There are also spinners of pearl, and aluminum, in the natural and the black finishes. Some are supplied with flutings to increase the reflecting surface.

Theoretically, the red and white enamel and nickel are for water of ordinary clearness; the black, aluminum, all white enamel, and pearl for very clear water, and the gold and silver for "dark" waters.

Sizes of spoons are designated by numbers, but there seems to be no established system, as different styles and makes of the same number vary considerably. In ordering by mail it is best to specify the size in inches. The proper sizes to use for the different fish depends a great deal on the character and condition of water, the style and finish of spoon, but for average conditions those measuring under one inch are for trout, crappies, rock bass, and other small fish; from one to two and one-eighth inches for bass and pickerel; from two to two and one-half inches for pike, and from two to three inches for muskellunge.

It may be a matter of interest, however, to know that a fourteen year old girl once landed a 35-pound "muskie" on a number one Skinner spoon.

For a long time spoons were used with plain single hooks; then someone conceived the idea of using a treble hook concealed in a tuft of feathers, but the tendency now is toward the single hook again. Few casters use the hook only but add a minnow, a frog, a strip of pork, or a single hook fly. The spinner with minnow or fly is the most popular for fishing fast water, but in large slow streams or weedy lakes the addition of a strip of pork is considered a help.

As to flies, when the solid colors are wanted the bucktails are recommended as they do not mat down or bedraggle like the feathered ones and they last longer. A feathered red Ibis fly with turned wings to act as weed guard is very popular with casters who fish weedy waters; the weedless bucktail is also good. In selecting weedless hooks with wire weed guards avoid those with very stiff guards. They are weedless no doubt—also fishless. Ordinary eyed or ringed bass flies are also useful. Let most of your selection be well-colored or "contrasty" patterns such as: Silver Doctor, Red Ibis, Parmechenee Belle, Yellow May, Col Fuller, Jungle Cock. A dark pattern or two —Black Gnat, Lord Baltimore, etc.—might be added for the sake of variety.

Most spinners are made with a snap safety pin fastening so that flies may be changed quickly and easily and this kind is what the caster needs. With a few of these and three or four flies one can readily make up combinations to suit any condition.

Ordinarily a spinner or spinner and fly is too light to cast on a short rod so it is customary to add a swivel dipsey sinker for extra weight. Personally we use both the double and single spinners, although there seems to be little difference in their effectiveness. The double type is supposed to imitate more closely a swimming minnow, but the single possesses the advantage of being simpler and cheaper; also some casters are of the opinion that with the double spinner the fish often strike at the upper blade and miss the hook. A new design avoids this by having a spinner on the end of each weed guard which brings them alongside the hook. Spinners have the reputation in some localities of being better for small mouth bass than the other variety, but this is more likely due to the fact that the spinner is more often used in streams, the natural habitat of the small mouth.

PORK RIND

Pork rind in some form or other is probably the bait most used by wielders of the short rod who fish in weedy places. This is especially true in the Middle West.

Game fish have no particular appetite for pork. Its success as a bait is due to the fact that it is white, it has an enticing flexibility or wriggle when in the water in the strip form, the fish do not eject it from the mouth as soon as it is struck because it is edible, and, finally, owing to the tough rind, it can not be pulled from the hook.

Pork rind is used in a great many ways. It can be bought at the tackle stores in strips, chunks, and "hams," and it is used mostly in these forms. The strips are about three inches in length and about half an inch wide at the upper end, tapering gradually to a point at the lower end. In this form it is very deadly as it possesses a snake-like movement in the water that is irresistible to the average game fish.

The strip is mostly used with a small single or tandem spinner and a fly—usually a weedless red Ibis. The spinner gives a fin-like movement, the fly mats down on the pork, the latter wriggles, and the whole lay-out bears a close resemblance to a crippled minnow, whose head is "all over blood" as a small boy would say, which is a choice morsel to any game fish. This spinner, fly, and pork strip combination is, of course, used mostly as an underwater bait, and will be practically weedless. For casting up to the edge of weed-beds and in the pockets it has few equals. In addition to the regular spinner and fly combination, there are also a number of very ingenious hooks made especially for pork rind.

The strip that is sold in bottles is much better than that packed in salt and sold in boxes as it has more wriggle; it is also superior to any that you can cut yourself as it is cut by special machinery and the preserving liquid not only preserves but adds to its flexibility. One of its chief merits from the standpoint of economy is the fact that a strip or two will usually be good for a full day's fishing.

Chunks and hams are made wedge-shape with high fronts to create a disturbance on the water and are used as surface baits. Sometimes the fish get into the lily pads, spatterdocks, and other weeds and refuse to be coaxed out. There is just one answer to this problem: a pork chunk or ham on a good weedless hook. In the Middle West the use of the pork chunk is considered by many to be the most artistic form of bait casting—if one may speak of art and pork at the same time. The directions given for using surface baits will apply also to the pork chunk. The idea in casting a chunk is to make it land on the water with not too much commotion, to start it back quickly without "skipping" it, and to keep it on the surface during the entire retrieve. It is usually cast halfway between the overhead and side cast.

It is a common practice among casters to cut their own pork on special models of more or less merit. For this purpose use dry salt pork. Remove all lean meat as only the fat is used. Always cut each piece with rind on one side, preferably the top. A sharp razor or thin-bladed knife is necessary for this work.

A favorite design to be used under water is the arrow-head or a thin wedge-shaped piece with "swaller" tails. It is used on a weedless hook with or without a spinner. Similar to this is the frog-shaped. This is cut in the outline of a frog with the hind legs outstretched. Some casters put a toothpick or sharpened stick between the "legs," wedge fashion, to keep them from tangling up. Minnow-shaped pork is also popular.

It is customary when using pork to pierce it crosswise and insert a small pair of "wings" of red flannel which adds to the attractiveness. Red darning cotton is also good for decorating pork. A strand or two run through the upper end of a strip helps it greatly, especially when it is used without a fly. In fact, many experienced casters like a dash of red on any bait.

Gullet is often used the same as pork. Gullet is the thin, tough, white skin taken from the throat or "chin" of different fishes, usually the pickerel. With a sharp knife one simply follows around the jaw bone which yields a triangular piece of skin, shaped similar to an imperfect arrowhead. It is an excellent lure when used in combination with a spinner and fly. We suspect that when fresh it has an appealing odor to most game fish. Gullet can be carried in the pork bottle.

NATURAL BAIT

There are no fine-spun theories regarding the whys and wherefores of natural bait. Its use is founded on the world-old principle that fish must eat to live and as they spend a great part of their existence hunting for food the natural bait angler simply takes advantage of the fact.

From the well-advertised success of artificial baits there is danger of the novice in bait casting looking upon natural bait as old-fashioned and more or less useless. This, of course, is a mistake. Every experienced caster knows lakes and streams that are noted as "live bait waters," for the simple reason that in that particular locality natural bait is always more successful than the artificial. Besides the bait question is a seasonable one. In many places the fish prefer artificial bait one time of the year and live bait another. A well-known example is Lake Chautauqua, New York. Here, according to the local experts, the muskellunge strikes best on spoons in September and shows a decided preference for minnows later in the season.

Surely the caster who pins his faith to one style of bait, natural or artificial, is missing some good fishing; besides he is neglecting his education.

MINNOWS

The small fish's place in the general scheme of things apparently is to supply food for larger fish, so they are produced in enormous quantities. This is especially true of most minnows, which are not necessarily, as some folks believe, young fish, but a family of fishes known as *Cyprinidae*. The proper term for young fish is "fry."

The Cyprindiae family consists of about forty genera and one hundred and thirty species, some of which reach considerable size. The German carp and the gold fish are perhaps the best-known members of the minnow family. All the Cyprindiae breed in the spring. During the breeding season the males become highly colored in some species, and "break out" with small tubercles, usually on the nose.

The desired qualities of a bait minnow depends mostly on their brightness and, for ordinary bait casting or still fishing, their vitality or ability to keep lively while on the hook and naturally those from fast water excel in these respects. In this class we have the fall fish (*Semotilus corporalis*) and the creek chub (*S. atromaculatus*) and the river chub (*Hybopsis kentuckiensis*). Other species well liked by both fish and fisherman are Store's chub (*H. Storiensis*) red fin or silverside (*Notropsis cornutus*), spottail shiner (*N. hudsoniensis*), silverside (*N. Whipplii*), slender silverside (*N. Atherinoids*), and blunt nose minnows (*Pimephales notatus*).

As a rule anglers classify all these minnows as either chubs or shiners and the men who sell minnows at most fishing resorts are even broader than that and include among their best sellers skip jacks (*Lobdesthes sicculus*), mud minnows (*Umbra limi*), commonly and wrongly called "young dogfish," the fry of yellow perch, pike-perch, and even black bass. On some streams young catfish or "mud cats" are very successful for bass. These are great favorites on the Susquehanna and other Eastern rivers.

On short trips to "civilized" waters when time is

valuable, the fisherman will usually buy his minnows, although it is a good plan to find out in advance whether or not they will be obtainable. Sometimes it will be necessary or desirable to catch them yourself which is usually a simple problem.

On large bodies of water without surface inlet or outlet or on big streams minnows will usually be found in sheltered spots and can be taken with a minnow net. One that folds umbrella-fashion is very handy. Bait it with bread or cracker crumbs when the minnows are near the surface, or fasten it to a long handle with strong cord, cast it out, and bring in quickly when the minnows are down deeper. Usually the most common lake minnows are spot-tailed shiners and they are good for both bass and pickerel. The outlets or inlets of large lakes are good places to catch bait, as the minnows have a habit of running in and out of these places.

Seining is the best way to catch minnows in small streams, but be sure your seine complies with the law, Some states limit the length and regulate the mesh of minnow seines. Creek chubs and river chubs are two of the very best minnows for bass. When they are in shallow water the best way to get them is to wade, lift your feet high as you move along, and drop each foot heavily on the water. This scares the minnows and they will seek refuge under a stone. Then dropping another stone on the one Mr. Minnow is under will stun him. Pick him up at once because they are tough and revive quickly. Minnow traps are useful around a permanent camp, as they work while you sleep or fish. They are usually baited with crumbs or pellets of dough.

Building a barricade of stones or stretching pieces of netting across narrow streams and driving the minnows into a grain sack in the center held open by a hoop sometimes gets bait in quantities and quickly. On deep water lakes and streams where netting and seining are difficult, large chubs can be taken on a tiny hook, sizes 14 to 18, baited with a maggot, or a small piece of worm.

Minnows are usually easier to catch very early or very late in the season, as then they are in the small feeder creeks. The "plant" of one of the large packers of prepared minnows in the Middle West is simply a small stream that empties into Lake Michigan. In the spring and fall they catch and prepare hundreds of thousands of minnows for bait.

For ordinary bait or still fishing, dead or prepared minnows cannot compare with live ones, but for casting they are apparently as good. Those who live in regions where there is usually a minnow famine may find it advisable to preserve some when they are plentiful. Simply pack them in bottles or jars that can be sealed tightly and pour over them a solution made by adding one part of formalin to four parts of water. A saturate (all the water will take up) solution of boracic acid is also good. You will find that scaling a dead minnow will add to its flexibility and attractiveness.

by the kind and size of fish likely to be caught. For bass and pickerel sizes 1-0 to 4-0 in the sproat shape and 22 to 18 in Cincinnati bass would be about right.

For game fish use good-sized minnows. One four to six inches is none to large for bass and from four to seven inches for pickerel or pike. A large bait is more easily seen by the fish and its size gives casting weight.

Either prepared or dead minnows are often used successfully with a device made for the purpose, such as the Archer spinner, and in rapid streams they are sometimes very attractive when threaded on the shank of a plain hook so they are curved and will spin in the water. Spoons and spinners improve a dead minnow more than they do a live one.

If a spinner is used with a live minnow it should be of light weight. For use with large minnows few spoons equal the old favorite Delavan although the cheap spear point hooks that come with it should be replaced by better ones. This spoon is supplied with two hooks, and a minnow is used on each. The method of baiting is to put the hook in at the minnow's mouth, out through the gills, then inserting the point near the tail. This is a good method for large minnows generally.

Ordinarily the minnow is best in water fairly clear of weeds, and this is fortunate because it enables the caster to use light tackle. With a short stiff rod there is always the probability of snapping off the minnow or whipping the life out of it. We doubt if

the Henshall rod will ever be improved upon for minnow casting.

FROGS

The motto of three famous literary characters: "One
for all; all for one," could well be applied to the
short rod, the large mouth bass, and the frog. They
make a winning combination, because the frog is
the natural prey of the large mouth bass, as well as
members of the pike family. These fish usually frequent weedy spots and such are the logical places to
use a short rod.

Frogs are usually hooked through both lips, from
below, the same as minnows, although we know casters
who are very successful in casting them head first.

There are many good special frog hooks and harnesses on the market. These special hooks (see any tackle
catalog) usually have a small upper hook with weed
guard, very similar to those used with minnow harnesses. The frog is hooked through the lips to this
small hook so that he straddles the actual hook. They
are made with and without spinners, and where the
weeds are not too thick the spinner is no doubt an
added attraction. When plain hooks are used, it is
a good plan to lash the frog securely to the shank
of the hook with a rubber band. A "belly down"
weight or keel sinker should be used with a plain hook
to make the frog ride right side up in the water. Most
special frog hooks and harnesses are provided with
these.

Just how deep to fish with a frog depends on cir-

cumstances. This can be determined by experimenting. When used in very heavy weed growth a frog
is usually kept close to or on the surface. This is
regulated by the speed of reeling. Sometimes best
results will be had by using a frog the same as a surface or a semi-surface bait, making short frequent
casts, varying the speed of retrieving, or alternately
reeling and stopping. When fishing this way it is best
to follow Father Isaac's advice and use the frog as
though you loved him. That is, to prevent unnecessary suffering, kill him before you put him on the
hook.

When fishing in clear water or in the deep holes
in midsummer, a live frog is better. Making long
casts, allowing the frog to settle, and reeling slowly
gets the most strikes then.

All varieties of frogs seem to be successful as baits
and the best rule to follow is to use the species native
to the region you are fishing. A frog weighing from
three-eights to three-quarters of an ounce is the best
size.

Personally, we have never had much success with
the artificial frogs, although in some waters they doubt-
less take fish.

The average fisherman will usually find it more
convenient to buy frogs from the tackle dealer, the
bait store, or small boy. They are best caught at
night with the aid of a lamp of some kind, which
should have a good reflector. A strong light blinds a
frog and when thus blinded he is easily caught.

Frogs can be carried in an old stocking, but the net bags made for the purpose are better. For large quantities, baskets with a cloth cover and an elastic opening are convenient. Frogs require little if any care, which is a point that recommends them to most fisherman. Where a large supply is kept on hand they can be cooped in a screened enclosure, and the contents of a fly-trap emptied into it from time to time will keep them in good condition.

Those living in states where very early fishing is permitted may find it worth while to provide a deep box full of mud and to permit a supply of late caught frogs to winter there.

Besides requiring little care the frog possesses nearly all the advantages of artificial baits, such as size, weight, and color and he is a dandy fare for nearly all game fish, especially large size specimens. He will give a good account of himself even in the hands of a beginner, although best results naturally come with practice.

CRAWFISH

Just as the frog is the staple diet of the large mouth bass, the small mouth's staff of life, when obtainable, is the crawfish or fresh-water crab. Although mostly used for bait fishing or still fishing the crawfish makes a good casting bait, under certain conditions, if properly handled. Long-shanked hooks are best and the craw can either be hooked through the tail or, better still, lashed to the hook's shank by a rubber band so that his head rests in the bend of the hook. Remember, a crawfish travels backwards.

Soft shell crabs are not a separate species. They are simply ordinary ones changing coats and that they are soft is due to the fact that the new shell has not had time to harden. "Soft shells" should always be used with a rubber band, otherwise they are likely to be jerked from the hook when a cast is made.

Crawfish are usually used as a small mouth lure and this means in most cases stream fishing. They can only be used for casting when the water is clear and even then a spinner usually helps to attract the fish to them as they are naturally not very conspicuous.

OTHER NATURAL BAITS

Worms are seldom used for casting, although a generous "gob" of them behind a spinner and retrieved slowly when the fish are feeding deep is a good bass bait and almost irresistible to pickerel. Another fish susceptible to this lure is the channel catfish, one of the very best of food fishes and incidentally a hard and persistent fighter.

Worms should be dug about a week before using and then "scoured" to be at their best. This is done by washing them and putting them in a jar or box in damp moss and leaving them there for a week. This removes all earthy matter and toughens them, to say nothing of making them cleaner to handle. They can be carried in damp sand.

The black-headed worm, which can be identified by the absence of the knot on the body, is the best worm. It is found in good garden soil. The "night crawler" is also good.

Mice, especially young field mice, are excellent bass and pickerel baits, but using animals as highly organized as mice strikes us as being cold-blooded. They are especially good along wooded shores and for casting under over-hanging banks, particularly after a rain. There is an artificial mouse covered with real mouse fur and equipped with a single hook that is often successful under these conditions; mouse colored plugs are also obtainable.

The helgramite, dobson, or grampus, is the larvae of the horned Corydalis. It is a dirty brown in color, and has three pairs of legs and a number of leg-like hairs on the sides of its body. It is found around old piers and under flat stones in the riffles of a stream. It is caught by raising the stone and holding a landing net so the current will carry it in. Helgramites can be kept indefinitely in damp, rotten wood. The helgramite is an excellent bass bait for bait fishing in rapid or shallow water, but is too small and inconspicuous for casting under ordinary conditions. However, it can be used very successfully at times with a small spinner to which two hooks and two helgramites are attached.

Just how many lures to carry on a fishing trip can be learned only by experience. We know a caster who uses only two baits: the spinner, red fly, pork strip combination and pork chunk in the lily pads. He is very successful. Another expert of our acquaintance seldom uses anything but live frogs. Still another, also a fishgetter, carries just three artificials. Continually changing baits is poor fishing strategy and the wise caster has a few favorites which he uses the greater part of the time, changing only to meet new conditions.

CHAPTER VIII

THE CASTER'S QUARRY

THE BLACK BASS

"THE black bass is eminently an American fish; he has the faculty of asserting himself and making himself completely at home wherever placed. He is plucky, game, brave, and unyielding to the last when hooked. He has the arrowy rush of the trout, the untiring strength and bold leap of the salmon, while he has a system of fighting tactics peculiarly his own. He will rise to the artificial fly as readily as the salmon or the brook trout under the same conditions; and will take the live minnow or other live bait under any and all circumstances favorable to the taking of any other fish. I consider him inch for inch and pound for pound the gamest fish that swims."

When Dr. Henshall, back in the seventies, made the above statement concerning the black bass he created quite a stir among the anglers of the day. Then the bass was little known as a game fish and there was no tackle to speak of suitable for bass fishing. Now, two-thirds of all fishermen are bass fishermen and two-thirds of all tackle made in this country is black bass tackle.

The fact that the black bass is the game fish of the people is due to his adaptability. He thrives, one variety or the other, in practically any kind of water, and in spite of the fact that he can not be propagated artificially, he is now found in every state of the Union, in nearly all parts of Canada, and in many places in Europe. He prospers under conditions that would be impossible for other game fishes. If absolute fearlessness in attacking living, or seemingly living, objects that move on or beneath the surface of the water constitutes gameness, then the black bass has no rival as a game fish.

The black bass family is divided into two varieties, the small mouth (*Micropterous Dolomieu*), and the large mouth (*Micropterous Salmoides*).

The former is the more aristocratic, thriving best in cool waters with gravelly or rocky bottom and running streams and feeds mostly on crawfish and minnows. The large mouth is not so particular and, is more often found in warmer, weedier spots, such as shallow lakes, slow streams, and ponds. Naturally he feeds on the food common to such places like frogs, warm water minnows, and small crustaceans.

Some anglers seem to have difficulty in distinguishing the two varieties, although no trouble should be had in identifying them when the differences are understood. As their names suggest, the principal difference is in the size of the mouth. In the large mouth variety, the mouth extends back of the eye, while in the small mouth variety it does not come quite to the eye.

The eye of the small mouth frequently shows some red, although this can not always be relied upon. The large mouth always has a pronounced "dent" in the forehead, while the small mouth's forehead is well-rounded. The small mouth is usually a trimmer fish, not so stoutly built as the large mouth, and his tail is not quite so square nor is his jaw so "undershot."

However, the best means of identifying the two species is by the scales. The scales of the small mouth are smaller and he has eleven rows of them above the median line (the dark streak or line running along the sides of most fishes) while the large mouth has only eight. The base of the small mouth's dorsal (back) fins are scaled; the large mouth's are bare. The small mouth has seventeen rows of scales on the cheek; the large mouth about ten. Both varieties often have a "musk-like" odor when taken from the water, but this is usually more pronounced in the small mouth variety.

The color of both varieties differs greatly, not only in different waters but in different individuals, the range being from pale yellow through different shades of green and yellow-bronze to dark almost black-green. Both species show dark transverse or longitudinal markings on the sides, especially in younger specimens; these markings occur more frequently on the large mouth species.

There is a great difference of opinion among anglers as to the relative gameness of the two varieties. Our personal opinion is that the difference is greatly exaggerated. The small mouth is a faster fish and a better leaper, but the large mouth is stronger and heavier for his age. When taken from the same waters little difference will be noted between them, although this is hardly a just comparison as the small mouth will usually be taken from the colder portions of the lake or stream. The small mouth's reputation as a fighter has also been favored by the fact that he is usually taken from fast water where the angler must not only fight against the fish but against the "pull" of the stream as well. We would rather catch small mouth bass, but we consider the large mouth the more valuable fish of the two because of his greater adaptability and more general distribution.

Bass spawn in the spring, as early as March in the South and as late as July in the far North. The weather and the character of the water have much to do with the spawning time. For instance, in Lake Como, a shallow weedy lake in southern Wisconsin, we have observed bass spawning three weeks before they started at Lake Geneva, a deep cold lake. Geographically, these waters are only a few miles apart.

Fortunately, black bass are very prolific. A female will frequently yield as much as twenty-five per cent of her weight in eggs. Large mouth bass spawn in marshy spots usually and build their nests on the roots of aquatic plants or will construct one of small sticks, while the small mouth scoops out a nest in the gravel or sand.

The courtship of the black bass is very interesting. The nest is always made by the male fish a week or so before he sallies forth to court "ye ladie faire." After the nest is finished, he approaches the female and "shows off," cutting capers the same way that a cock bird does in courting a hen. Meanwhile, he is coaxing or driving the female toward his nest. Naturally, she appears shy and reluctant. When he gets her to the nest he immediately ascertains whether or not she is "ripe." If not, he immediately drives her away and seeks another mate. If ripe, the more serious business of egg-laying takes place. Each fish swims in opposite directions, rubbing bellies as they pass, and as the female ejects the eggs the male fertilizes them.

Sometimes it is difficult to get the eggs started and we have often observed the male fish nipping the belly of the female while the latter trembles and twists its body about as though to loosen the tissues. The eggs are not all laid at the same time, it usually taking about two days to complete the function.

After the eggs are laid the female leaves the nest and the male lies over them to drive off marauders, and fans continually with fins and tail to prevent sediment or dirt settling in the nest which interferes with the hatch. Incidentally, motor boats should not be run near the spawning beds during the hatching season on account of the dirt they stir up.

While the parent fish is guarding the nest it does not feed, but will attack anything coming into the vicinity, and in some parts of the country unscrupulous fishermen take advantage of this fact by dropping their baits on the spawning beds.

The eggs hatch on an average in about ten days and as the young are not supplied with a large yolk sac like the fry of most fishes they are helpless for about the first week. This is why it is doubly a crime to catch parent fish during the nesting season. The young feed on small crustaceas, and other minute organisms and reach about five inches in length the first year and about a pound in weight the second. Thereafter they gain about a pound a year under favorable conditions.

The maximum normal weight.for small mouth bass is about five pounds; for large mouth in northern waters about seven pounds. Those that exceed these weights are "freaks" and are not nearly as plentiful as fishermen's yarns would lead one to believe.

The growth of fish depends on the abundance of food, the temperature of the water, and the extent of range, the latter being apparently the most important. At any rate, bass from large bodies of water are always larger than those of equal age taken from smaller areas. In small ponds, under natural conditions, bass grow very slowly, sometimes not at all. In the South where food is plentiful and the fish do not hibernate in the winter the large mouth bass has been known to reach twenty pounds in weight. The largest small mouth bass we know of weighed ten and one-fourth pounds.

The habits of the black bass vary greatly under different circumstances, local conditions exerting a greater influence than is generally supposed. The general habits of different fishes and their relation to fisherman's luck will be discussed in a later chapter.

PIKE AND PICKEREL

The terms pike and pickerel are used so indiscriminately that there is considerable confusion regarding the classification of these fishes among anglers, although not among ichthyologists.

The pickerel of the Middle West (*Esox lucius*) is the true pike, large specimens of which are sometimes given the high-sounding name of Great Northern Pike —although this title is also bestowed on certain species, or probably sub-species, of the muskellunge. The only true pickerel native to the waters west of the Alleghenies is the western pickerel (*Esox vermiculatur*); he is generally known as "grass pike" and seldom exceeds a foot in length.

The pike is found in this country from the Ohio river northward, in Alaska, in nearly all parts of Canada, where it is called jack-fish, and is especially abundant in the Great Lakes region and in the small lakes of the upper Mississippi valley. It is also common in Europe and Asia.

In color the pike is a bluish or greenish-gray on the

back with lighter sides and silvery white on the under part, with many white or yellow bean-shaped spots always lighter than the ground color. Fins and tail are marked with dark spots or blotches. As with all members of the family the anal and dorsal fins are on a vertical line. The head is about one-fourth the length of the body, the nose is flattened, alligator-like, and the mouth is armed with long sharp teeth on both jaws while the roof of the mouth bristles with a villainous lot of teeth all curving backward. It breeds in early spring a little later than the pike-perch.

The formidable array of teeth and the cold, cruel look in his eye do not belie the pike's true nature. He is a free-booter who lies under cover of the weeds and snaps up any fish, frog, acquatic bird, mouse, dragon-fly, or crustacea that passes his way. They are very greedy and you will sometimes catch one with the tail of a still undigested fish protruding from its mouth, which leads one to suspect that they kill simply for the sake of killing. Even his own kind are not spared—he is a cannibal. The pike is found mostly in shallow weedy lakes, in the slower streams, or in the slower weedy portions of large bodies of water.

The average weight of the pike is probably around three pounds, although specimens of forty pounds and over have been taken. Pike weighing eight and ten pounds are not uncommon.

As a food and game fish the pike varies greatly in different waters. When taken from cold water, he is a fairly good table fish, although full of small bones.

Under these conditions he usually puts up a valiant fight, for a short time at least, and is a game fish in every sense of the word.

In some parts of the country, especially in Wisconsin and Minnesota, he is known as a "snake." In these regions he is under-fed (despite his efficient appearance he can not stand much competition) and consists mostly of head; will strike at anything in the bait line, much to the disgust of muskellunge and bass fishermen, and is generally known as a pest of the first class.

The western pickerel (*Esox vermiculatur*) seldom exceeds a foot in length, and is common in the upper and middle Mississippi valleys and the Great Lakes region and in streams tributary to lakes Michigan and Erie. It prefers weedy, sluggish waters ,and because of its small size is not of much importance.

The eastern pickerel (*Esox reticulatur*) sometimes called green pike and chain pickerel, is found in all the states east of the Alleghenies. It resembles the pike in general appearance, although it seldom if ever reaches over eight pounds in weight. Its color is greenish, with a golden lustre on the sides and with lighter underparts. The markings on the sides form a chain-like network. There is a dark spot below the eye. In some parts of its range it is a game fish of considerable importance.

The banded pickerel (*Esox Americanus*) is found in nearly all of the streams east of the Alleghenies, but is of small importance to the angler.

From the fisherman's standpoint, there is no difference between the above-mentioned members of the pike family, except in size.

THE MUSKELLUNGE

The muskellunge (*Esox nobiliar* or *E. Masquinongy*) known also by a dozen or more similar names, but called the "muskie" by most fishermen, is the most important member of the pike family. He is found in Canada, in the Great Lakes and tributary waters, the upper St. Lawrence River, and certain lakes in Wisconsin and Minnesota. In the latter places and among the Thousand Isles he seems to be the most plentiful.

Another variety, the Chautauqua muskellunge, (*Esox Ohiensis*), is known chiefly from Lake Chautauqua, certain streams in Ohio, and at one time was common in the Ohio River and some of its tributaries.

The muskellunge reaches a length of seven or eight feet and a weight of eighty pounds or more. The average weight is from eight to ten pounds. This is considerably less than is generally supposed by those who never see a "muskie" except when mounted, but one must remember that for every thirty pounder one sees mounted, a dozen or more smaller ones are caught and are either eaten or thrown back. Only the good-sized specimens reach the taxidermists.

The habits of the muskellunge are very similar to those of the pike. He is a solitary fish who hides in the weeds and preys on smaller fish of all kinds, frogs, small rodents, birds, snakes, etc. Like the pike he is usually found on the edge of weed-beds in water from five to twelve feet deep, or in streams he often hides behind sunken logs, fallen trees, boulders, and shelving banks. They are also taken in lakes in the vicinity of gravel bars or in water with gravel bottoms covered with short gassy weeds. They spawn early in the spring.

The muskellunge usually feed in the morning and at evening. During the spring, in the breeding season, he is a gallant lover and then you will usually find them in pairs, and when one is hooked, the other will frequently show itself. In midsummer, usually in August, they seem to have trouble with their teeth, and will frequently follow a bait without touching it, or strike it very gingerly. Whether this condition is a disease, or whether they are simply changing or growing new teeth is a much-debated question. In fact, owing to his natural shyness, the muskellunge is a difficult fish to study, and considering their importance we 'have little positive knowledge about them.

There are also no well-defined standards of classification, as there is much variation in specimens from certain waters in Minnesota and Wisconsin. One of our standard authorities (Jordan and Everman) mentions the unspotted muskellunge under the heading "Great Northern Pike" (*Esox immasculatus,* Gerard) but have only the following to say: "This muskellunge is known only from Eagle Lake and other small lakes in Wisconsin and Minnesota. From the Great Lakes muskellunge it differs in having the body entirely unspotted or with vague dark cross-shades. The tail is a little more slender and the fins a little higher. This form has not been studied critically and its relation to *E. masquinongy* and *E. ohiensis* have not been clearly made out."

Specimens showing the dark cross-shades are usually called "tiger muskellunge."

The muskellunge is usually caught by trolling, but the practice of catching him by casting with a short rod is growing. A rather heavy rod should be used, a good steel one probably being the best for this work for the average caster. A hard-braid or cored line testing twenty or twenty-two pounds will be about right, owing to the fact that rather heavy lures will be employed. For bait, a large chub or fall-fish, black sucker, live frog, or medium-size spoon with either plain hook or bucktail are the favorites.

Hooks must be of good size and of the best quality, and when a spoon is not used a heavy wire leader or trace will often prevent the fish escaping.

As a game fish the muskellunge ranks high; not alone because of his size, but he is a hard, tricky fighter; a magnificent leaper, who usually strikes the lure savagely upwards from the side, often clearing the water with a great leap when he does so. For the table the muskellunge is better than the pike, and his flesh improves after being kept a day or two on ice.

Pike, pickerel, and muskellunge can be distinguished

by the following formula: Pike—Cheeks entirely scaled but only upper half of gill covered; lower half naked. Spots always lighter than ground color. Pickerel—Both cheeks and gill covers entirely scaled.

Muskellunge—Upper part of cheeks and gill covers scaled; lower half naked. If spotted, spots are always darker than ground color.

THE PIKE-PERCH

This fish is known by a number of names, such as wall-eyed pike, pickerel, yellow pike, blue pike, dore, jacksalmon, okow, and blow fish, but the term pike-perch is the most appropriate because it designates its pike-like form and it is a member of the perch family.

This fish is widely distributed, being found throughout the Great Lakes region, in several streams east of the Alleghenies, in small lakes in New York, and in many lakes and streams in the Mississippi valley. Commercially it is most abundant in Lake Erie, where, strange to say, it is called "pickerel." It is olive brown yellow or dull blue in color, with lighter underparts. Its eye is large and glassy. It ranks among the very best as a food fish, its flesh being white, flaky, and of a fine flavor.

The pike-perch inhabits deep cold water and prefers gravelly or rocky bottom. In lakes, it will usually be found in the deep pools or near spring holes, while on the stream its favorite feeding-places are at the foot of the rapids, below dams, log-jams, etc.

On cloudy days and at evening it will often rise
well to the fly, but the best casting bait is a minnow
or crawfish. It is a night feeder, as can be guessed
from the size and appearance of its eyes, and frequently they can be taken on moonlight nights with
artificial baits like a small-bodied underwater plug,
white or aluminum in color, by casting on the bars in
lakes or near rapids and dams in streams.

The pike-perch spawns very early in the spring,
usually before the ice is gone, and prefers gravel bottom for the purpose. A two-pound fish will produce
about ninety thousand eggs. The young grow quite
rapidly. The average weight of the pike-perch is
around two or three pounds, although they probably
reach a weight of twenty pounds or over. One of
twelve or fifteen pounds is a large specimen.

In lake fishing, pike-perch are caught mostly in the
spring or midsummer, while on the stream the best
time seems to be in the fall after the first light frost.
They do not strike with the savage rush of the bass
or muskellunge and as fighters they rank only fair.

OTHER FISHES

The black bass, because of his sterling qualities and
wide distribution, is the principal quarry of the bait
caster, but in most bass waters other species co-exist.
These are most frequently the pike, pickerel, pike-
perch, and muskellunge, although other fishes, like
the rock bass and croppie, often strike the caster's

lure, but it is seldom one goes out after these "li'l fellers." It can be done, however, simply by using smaller baits, but the artistic way to catch "pan fish" is to use a light fly-rod and flies on Nos. 14 and 16 hooks.

The channel or speckled catfish (*Ictalurus puncta-tus*), unlike other catfish, prefers running water, is a clean feeder, and an excellent food fish. He will frequently strike at a minnow or a spinner baited with worms, or a spinner with a white bucktail fly if it is permitted to sink and is retrieved slowly.

CHAPTER IX

HINTS ON FISHING

FISHING A BIG LAKE

THE "know how" of fishing consists of knowing where the fish are, selecting the bait accordingly, presenting it in a tempting way, and finally landing the fish. It is a subject that few angling writers attempt to write about, due mostly to the fact that one can only generalize because conditions vary so. It is well that this is true because as soon as fishing is reduced to a formula, to established rules-of-thumb, it ceases to be a sport—remove the element of chance and you have nothing left.

Scientific angling is not likely to appeal to ultra-conservative people. It is for the man with quite a bit of boy in his make-up, a dash of adventure, a tincture of gambling, a man with the same spirit that moves a prospector to load a pick and shovel on a burro's back and travel out into the deserts and mountains in the never-ending search for "the big strike." Scientific angling is for folks who believe with Robert Louis Stevenson that it is better far to travel than it is to arrive, or, to bring it nearer home, who believe

138

that it is better far to fish than to merely catch fish.

However, hope long deferred makes a disgusted fisherman, and a reasonable number of strikes and fish is necessary to the angler's happiness. To get these requires some luck, some knowledge of fish and waters, some idea of the general rules of the game, and the latter is all any writer can hope to impart. The person who takes up bait casting must be something of a student, and as he progresses he will find the greatest pleasure of fishing is to work out his own problems as they arise.

The main attractions to fish are water of equable temperature and food, and this fact should always be kept in mind by anglers fishing strange waters. For this reason, very early in the season fish are more likely to be found in the shallower water, because shallow water warms more quickly and therefore the weeds begin to grow sooner. The high temperature warms the larvae of insects, dormant crustacea, and other creatures into life and the minnows are usually attracted to such places to feed on the crustacea (minute shrimp-like or crab-like organisms such as water lice, etc.) and these crustacea and minnows are the staff of life of all game fishes. It is very simple.

So the first place to try on a big lake in the early season is the shallow, weedy portion. These places on large lakes will often be found near the inlet or outlet if they are surface fed or surface drained.

For shallow water fishing, especially for bass, nothing quite equals a surface bait of some kind. This can be an artificial bait or a frog, or, if the water is very weedy, a pork chunk on a weedless hook. Directions for handling these baits are given in previous chapters.

Wobblers are also effective when cast up to the edge of the weeds, and the same may be said of the spinner, fly, and pork strip combination or other spinning baits. These baits are also very taking over submerged weed beds, which are favorite hunting grounds of game fish. See chapter on wobblers for directions for fishing under these conditions. Also try spots where feeder creeks of streams enter the lake as the fish are inclined to explore these places for food.

After the weeds have been tried thoroughly, give your attention to such places as old piers, fallen trees, rocks in shallow water, accumulations of driftwood, and sheltered spots generally.

On lakes where there are no weedy spots to speak of try the gravelly and sandy bars. On lakes of this kind, especially if they are of large area, it is always advisable to secure the services of a guide. If this cannot be done, the quickest way to learn the location of bars and ledges is to get the information from some "native." Usually the man who rents the boats or sells minnows or some other old-timer who makes his "livin' off'n the lake" knows but will not always part with the information readily. Sometimes a generous tip will help; at all times be diplomatic.

Keep your eye on the resident fishermen. They often are very able men when it comes to fishing. They have fished their own waters under all conditions and know "where they are at."

If it happens that no local talent is available, then you will have to do some prospecting on your own hook. Here is where a motor-boat or an out-board motor will prove a blessing. In any event, get a sounding line with a good weight on the end. Making a few soundings will often save hours of just fishing around. If possible, find out from someone who knows just how near normal the water is while you are there. High water marks on the shore, on stakes, piles, or docks will give you some idea of this. Enter your observations in a notebook for future reference.

The surface of any lake looks very much the same and once you have found a bar or reef "mark it down" by lining it up with some dissimilar objects on two shores. That is, so that if a straight line were drawn from each object to the marked-down spot they would intersect there. Sometimes you can also use your watch and compass to good advantage in re-finding a place of this kind. For instance, if you reach the edge of a reef by rowing at a normal gait for seven minutes and fourteen seconds northeast by east from a certain spot on shore to-day, you can find the same spot six months later by doing the same thing, making, of course, some allowance for wind. Particular attention should be paid to finding and marking down the edges and bars and reefs as these places will be needed later on.

Islands and points are usually the outcroppings of reefs and ledges, and the latter are almost always found near by. Shallow spots like these usually are small mouth bass water, and the absence of heavy weed growth gives you an opportunity to use light tackle. Minnows, spinners, and small wobblers are the baits most likely to get results under these conditions.

In the fore part of the season, warm, bright sunny days with just enough wind to make the sunbeams dance on the surface are best to bring out the fish to feed and play, and the best part of the day is when the sun is out.

As the weather and water gradually warm the fish move toward deeper water, and from late spring until midsummer they move about quite a bit. At this season they do most of their feeding early in the evening and early in the morning. Then they are in the shallow water usually near the outer or deep water edge of the weed beds and bars. Wobblers, spinner, and pork rind, frogs or minnows are the logical baits. Don't overlook the "pockets." If one wishes to fish all day during this season of the year the hours during which the sun is high, say from ten in the morning to four in the afternoon, fishing the deeper places, such as the shelf where the bottom drops off into deeper water, with minnows, frogs, and underwater baits will probably get the best results. At this time of the year the pike-perch will be found in fairly deep water with gravelly bottom or at the foot of dams if they are present, while the muskellunge will be hunting about on the outer edge of weed beds in water from ten to fifteen feet deep or in water farther out but of about the same depth with rocky or grassy bottom.

During midsummer, if the season has been warm the fish retire to the deep holes where the water is cool and at this time they are not in a "biting" mood as a rule. They come into the shallows late in the afternoon and are likely to remain there until sun-up the next morning, although the general belief is that they do little feeding from midnight until daylight.

Night fishing is often successful in midsummer. On shallow lakes where there are no deep cool pools or spring holes the fish seek the shade of over-hanging banks and thick weed growths. Casting up to the edge of the weeds with wobbler or pork strip, or going right into the weeds and pockets with pork chunk or frog is the most productive of results.

When there are deep pools, however, about the only way to get any fish to speak of is to get your bait down to them. This can be either a frog, a large minnow, or a small-bodied underwater plug with a swivel snap sinker ahead of it. Make long casts, allow the bait to sink, reel slowly, and strike hard is the system under these conditions. Large bass and pike-perch and very large members of the pike family are often taken from these deep holes. Smaller specimens are usually found in the submerged weed beds in fairly deep water—the big fellows drive them out of the choice spots. Pike-perch are sometimes taken in midsummer by casting over bars and reefs on moonlight nights.

Late in the summer the weeds begin to throw off their seeds, the water becomes cloudy, the fish seem lifeless and not at all inclined to strike. Gradually the water cools and the seed-spores settle to make the weed beds we will cast over next season. This is the time of year when "the bloom is off the water"; the fish take a new lease on life, and are hungry and full of fight. These conditions with the absence of mosquitoes and flies and the bracing weather with its Indian summer haze conspire to make autumn angling, in many respects, the best of all the year.

The fag end of the season toward the end of October in northern latitudes, has a few bright warm days, but by this time the shallow water cools quickly and the fish are retiring again to the deep holes where they pass the winter.

SMALL LAKES

Ordinarily the small lake is a simpler problem to the stranger. Small weedless lakes are in the minority because small lakes are favorable to weed-growth unless they are very deep. When we do meet with them it is simply a question of finding the shallow spots— the ledges, reefs, bars, and "shelf" and this is naturally easier than on a large body of water. Such lakes are usually small mouth bass waters unless fed or drained by a large, sedge lined stream or connecting with a larger lake or lakes. When this is the case don't overlook the point where the stream enters or the channel to the other waters.

The small, weedy lake will simply have to be "combed over," first, by fishing the edge of the weedy margin with frog, pork strip, or wobbler, getting about sixty feet out and casting in, or, if the water is not over four or five feet deep, a surface bait. One or two trips around will tell the story. Then if nothing in the strike line is forthcoming, drop your lure, which can be a frog, pork chunk, or some other weedless bait, right into the weeds. Often fairly open spots will be found between shore and weed margin and these are sometimes ideal fishing places. If the bottom is not too soft spots of this kind are best fished by wading from shore. Isolated clumps of rushes, spatterdock, or lilypads should be fished carefully.

Even very weedy lakes have at least a small portion of open water in the center. Explore it carefully with a sounding line, as the edge of a reef or rocky ledge in such a place. makes a jewel of a spot for fishing in midseason. Fishing the deep water is done the same as in a large lake.

LARGE SLOW STREAMS

Just as a large lake may be partly weedy and partly open a large stream may differ in certain parts, but for convenience we will assume that the large stream is simply a more or less weed-bordered river and will handle the swifter portions under the subject of small fast streams.

Such a stream will be fished either from shore or from a boat as they are often too deep to wade or the soft bottom prohibits this method. Fishing from shore is a favorite style with many casters in certain parts of the country. One simply walks along the banks as noislessly and as inconspicuously as possible, casting into the likely spots. If the stream is narrow enough to enable the caster to reach the opposite shore it is then a very deadly method. Strong tackle should be used when shore casting and especially must the line be good, as landing a fish under such circumstances is not always an easy proposition.

Floating down the stream, however, has much to recommend it. There is an indescribable charm in such fishing as every turn or bend of the stream presents new scenes, little gems of landscape, opportunities for nature study that you can get in no other way, not even by wading. As your boat drifts silently down with the flow you become a part of the stream and if you keep silent you will be accepted as one of the family by the river and wood folks you meet on your way.

Even the squirrels forget to chatter at you, the bluejays do not scold as they do when you invade their domain afoot, the turtles do not permit you to disturb their siestas—in short "you belong." Besides, coming back to the subject of fishing, you are always fishing new water and each new spot may be the lurking place of the "grand daddy of them all," that you know you are going to get some day.

It is best when fishing a stream from a boat to work in pairs, each alternately handling the paddle while the other fishes. Otherwise unless the flow is very sluggish you will be forced to pass by good spots.

In stream fishing the second man is often necessary as the fish has many things in its favor—there are many snags that cannot be seen and you must fight the flow of the stream as well as the strength of the fish.

The paddler or oarsman should be to the rear of the one casting, the boat should be moved noislessly (which recommends paddling or poling instead of rowing) and the skipper of the craft should keep the caster within easy casting distance of the good places such as the edge of the weed line, a clump of rushes or spatterdock, tangles of driftwood, jutting logs and rocks, fallen trees, stretches of over-hanging banks of foliage. By easy casting distance we would mean about forty to sixty feet.

Whenever a likely looking spot is found the paddler should if possible stop the boat by driving the paddle into the bottom or silently dropping the anchor until that spot is worked thoroughly. For example, in case of a log jutting its nose out of the water three or four casts along either side of it are none too many. In river fishing, when casting up to obstacles of this kind, the quick retrieve of the lure is necessary. When using an underwater lure it keeps it near the surface and prevents it connecting with some unseen snag and with any bait it gets the quiet impetuous strike that usually means a well-hooked fish.

On narrow streams it is best to work the good spots on either side, preference being given, of course, to the side where the current is the fastest, but on wide streams it is more business-like to work up one side and drift down the other.

Baits? Almost anything goes in river fishing, depending of course on circumstances—spinner and fly, frogs, pork, minnows, and even surface baits when the water is smooth. In the eddies made by a sharp turn of the river bed underwater baits are very successful. Both bass and pickerel will often be found in such places.

At the mouths of creeks entering the main stream you will usually find good fishing and in midsummer any place where the water is heavily shaded whether by trees or overhanging banks or cooled by springs should be worked carefully. If one fishes a strange stream and it connects with a lake near by, then the plot thickens, as the story books say. It may happen that the fish in the river seldom if ever enter the lake, but on the other hand the fish may show a decided preference for the lake and come into the river only occasionally, perhaps only to spawn. In a case of this kind, it is best to find out from some one who knows just what relation the lake bears to fishing in the river and vice-versa.

SMALL STREAMS

By small streams we mean a rapid flowing stream as distinguished from a slow somewhat weedy river discussed in the last chapter. Certain portions of a large stream, of course, may possess fast water or rapids and we will try to cover that phase of it in this chapter.

Fishing a strange stream is a man-sized job because success depends a great deal on the fishermen's knowledge of the stream's bed. Such knowledge of any stream cannot be gained in an hour or a day nor from a survey from the banks. You have to get right into the water and explore it, preferably during a low water period, with the help of your feet. In short, to know a stream you practically have to touch every foot of it with the soles of your boots.

Every boulder should be noted during low water and its exact location should be marked down and an entry made in your notebook—they make excellent fishing places when the water is normal and then they cannot be seen and are hard to locate. Piscatorially speaking, the typical fast water stream consists of three parts: the pools, the reaches, and the rapids.

Pools are mostly found at the foot of the rapids or at a turn in the bed of the stream. It is usually quiet water or if any motion is noticeable it is circular —what the small boys call "a slow whirlpool." If large and deep the pool is often the place for large fish and if pike and pickerel are native to the stream here is where you will find them as they do not naturally love fast water. The deep pools at the foot of rapids are the places to look for pike-perch in midsummer.

Reaches are stretches where the water runs deep and unbroken, such as the water between rapids, and while not fished as often as the pools they yield some fish, especially on cloudy days or during cool weather.

The rapids are ideal places for live bait, for if a fish is there he is usually feeding and is waiting for the fast water to bring a half-stunned minnow, craw, or helgramite into his retreat. The spots to look for fish when working the rapids are the little eddies around outcropping rocks, boulders, or other obstructions, for here is where the fish lie. Drop a few small chips into the stream and watch where they go. Food goes to the same places; see that your baits do also. Generally speaking, the rapids are at their best in spring or fall; the reaches in early summer; the deep holes in midsummer during warm weather, especially the pools where springs enter the stream.

When fishing an average fast stream it is usually done by wading and this is one of the most enjoyable methods of fishing. You get so close to the water-so intimate with the stream—that it soon becomes an old friend.

Whether to fish up stream or down stream is an old subject of debate among trout fishermen and there seems to be as much diversity of opinion among those who seek the bass. Bass, like trout, lie with their

heads up stream and there is the ever-present possibility of scaring the fish by casting down stream to
him. One seldom, however, fishes directly either up
or down stream but across stream at an angle. Usually in fishing a stream the writer prefers to cast down
and across, retrieving the lure partially against the
current, sometimes retrieving it a way and then permitting it to fall back again in 'imitation of a minnow
trying to breast the current. When using spinners
they work best when reeled against, or at least aross
the flow.

It is common advice that when a fish is hooked the
fisherman should lead him to a quiet spot and then
land him, which is good advice if it can be done. Our
experience is ·that it often is 'impracticable.

Small mouth bass are the usual quarry in fishing
a fast stream because fast water and rocky or gravelly
bottom are his favorite haunts, the large mouth bass
preferring slower water, mud bottom, and weeds as
do the pike and pickerel. Pike-perch are often found
in the same waters as the small mouth bass. Since
the small mouth bass and pike-perch are most often
found in the fast stream it naturally follows that their
favorite foods—stream minnows, crawfish, and helgramites—are the best natural baits. The spinner
and spinner and fly combination are also at their
best in fast water. The wobbler and underwater
artificial baits can be used in the deeper pools and
reaches.

As much as one may admire the short casting rod it must be confessed that the Henshall rod is a much better tool for fast water fishing.

NIGHT CASTING

All, or nearly all, game fishes are nocturnal in their habits. That is, they travel about and feed mostly at night and it is a generally accepted fact that the fish we catch in the daytime are those which, for some reason or other, did not satisfy their hunger the night before. Bass and the pikes are night feeders and they will often come to shore after nightfall to feed on minnows, frogs, crawfishes, etc., and it is not an uncommon experience to walk along the shores at night with a flashlight and see bass in water so shallow that their back fins show above the surface.

As regards bass, it will be found that the big old timer always secludes himself in the daytime and does most of his feeding at night only—that's how he got to be an old timer. It was a long time before casters, as a class, put these facts together, but now the sport of night casting is quite generally practiced.

While it seems to the writer that the sun is necessary for ideal fishing, one can not deny the fascination of a strike in the dark (sounds like the title of a melodrama, doesn't it?), and while the strikes are not as frequent and the percentage of fish landed is smaller than when fishing in the daytime, the uncertainty is an inducement in itself. Besides there is always the allurement of the possibility of landing a "whopper."

Fortunately, the best season of the year for night casting is in midsummer when fishing in the daytime is the least productive. This is the time that the fish, especially bass, spend their days in the deepest water and come into the shallows at, or immediately after, sundown. These facts should be kept in mind by those who take their vacations during the hot spell and by those who live near fishable waters and have little time during the day to fish.

The best water for this fishing is, of course, that which is free of heavy weeds, logs, and other obstructions, because you usually are unable to tell where your fish is going when hooked and he is therefore likely to foul your line if there is any debris in the immediate vicinity.

The tackle for night casting must be sturdy, not only because the fish are likely to be larger, but because it is impossible to handle a hooked fish delicately when you cannot see him. The rod should be of steel or wood, although a heavy bamboo one can be used, and the line should test from 16 to 20 pounds, fine casting of course being out of the question. Some very able casters use a self-thumbing reel for night work and there is no doubt that a back-lash and a big fish struggling for liberty way out there some place in the dark would be a very embarrassing combination!

Light colored lures are the best and those with the luminous finish are of especial value. Luminous finish is phosphorous, that "absorbs" light and throws it off in the dark, causing the bait to glow something like the dampened head of a parlor match.

Baits with this finish should not be exposed to the direct rays of the sun. Exposure a few hours to ordinary daylight or a half hour or so under the artificial light will bring out the glow enough for a night's casting. Many good surface baits are made with this finish for night fishing. Luminous baits can be washed with ordinary soap and water and they are also useful for fishing in the daytime.

Pork rind is also a good night bait, a little longer strip or larger chunk than ordinarily used can be employed. Silver, nickel, or white enamel spinners about two inches long (two and a half or three inches in the willow leaf design) with or without white bucktail or pork strip, large minnows, white wobblers, or frogs, are all successful night baits.

Rattling of oars or stamping of feet should be avoided, as quietness reigns supreme on the water at night. Row slowly and quietly and always cast toward shore if possible. Don't attempt long distance casting as you thereby invite back-lashes and always carry a flashlight or lantern so you can see to untangle those that do occur.

Cast across the shadow of the shore line if you can. Speed of reeling depends on circumstances, but the irregular style of retrieving, such as is often used with surface baits seems to be the most successful with us. That is, start the bait back quickly and fast, stop an instant, reel, stop, reel, and so on. If you hear anything like the swirl of a fish near your bait, strike immediately, don't wait to feel the "bite." Land your fish as quickly as possible and if he makes much of a struggle leave the spot for a while until things quiet down again.

It is a good plan to pick out a few likely spots in the daytime for night casting and study them to get an idea of the conditions.

Don't forget Mr. Night Caster, to provide yourself with some good mosquito "dope." A strong solution of Epsom salts, allowed to dry on the face and hands, is good.

ATTRACTING THE FISH

Very often in his traveling about, fishing different waters, the caster will run across lakes and streams that he knows contain many fish but that can seldom be induced to strike.

This condition can be due to several things. There may be such an abundance of natural food that the fish are overfed and sluggish, but more often it is due to the fact that the feeding grounds are quite extensive and the fish are widely distributed. This reduces competition and ordinarily competition is one of the best of strike inducers, the reason being that even a well-fed fish will snap up a piece of food if only to prevent some other fish getting it. Such conditions call for remedies that ordinarily would be beyond the pale of sportsmanship. The problem in a case of this kind is to get the fish together.

One method of attracting fish is to "bait" a certain piece of water. This is done by marking off a certain part of the lake or stream with buoys or stakes and in these confines throwing over cut-up fish, morsels of meat, dead minnows, worms, and other fish foods. Of course in doing this the proportion of small fry to sizeable game fish attracted is bound to be high.

A still better way is to build what one might call a "fish retreat." A good permanent retreat can be built of 2 x 2's or 2 x 4's. Take four pieces a little longer than the average depth of the water after making allowance for driving one end into the bottom. Paint them a bright red or scarlet, using good paint, preferably two coats. When they are dry, sharpen one end of each piece for driving.

Take two of these pieces and connect them with a cross-piece about eight feet long. This will give one half of the framework for the retreat which will be in the form of a capital H but with the cross-piece considerably below the center. With the other two pieces and another cross-piece the other half of the frame is made. Each half is then driven into the bottom or, in case of rocky bottom, is anchored with stones. They are placed about twelve or fifteen feet apart facing each other, and this is the foundation of the retreat.

Now cut some limbs from near-by trees (do not use conifers or evergreens) and sink them between your frames so that the heavy ends or butts are toward the center and the light or small ends are resting on the cross-pieces. The retreat is now finished but if any paint is left use it on some good-sized stones and drop them in the vicinity. The place to build your retreat depends a great deal on circumstances. As a general rule, the best place in a lake is near a point, just where the bottom drops off into deeper water or at the mouth of a tributary stream. On large streams build it near some deep pool and in fairly quiet water. The presence of motor-boats, hotels, and other things of course will influence your choice of spots.

The use of a scheme of this kind smacks too much of pot-fishing where the conditions are normal as it is surprising how soon a fish retreat will attract fish. They evidently see the bright colors from quite a distance and being naturally curious stop to investigate as they travel by. When they find a nice shady spot they stay, not only because of the shade but because a place of this kind attracts minnows and other food.

The very best place to cast over your retreat is right through the center and the heavy ends of the limbs are placed here, pointing slightly downward, so you will not get snagged on the foliage. You should work the retreat from all sides, however, being careful not to get snagged. If you do you will have to row up to release the hook and then it will be necessary to fish elsewhere for a while.

The retreat described above is permanent. All it needs each year is a new supply of foliage and it improves every season. The accumulation of twigs and the stones afford hiding and feeding places for minnows, crawfish, and other animal life.

For week-end trips simpler retreats can be rigged up with cane poles for uprights and cord or wire for cross-pieces.

HOOKING, PLAYING, AND LANDING THE FISH

After the angler has found the fish, selects the proper bait, and at last gets the strike that makes his heart "miss on one cylinder," there still remains the problem of hooking, playing, and landing the prize. As it is neither polite nor necessary to tell the experienced caster how to handle his fish, it is understood that this chapter is for the beginner who is somewhat skeptical as to the ability of what seems to him a fragile piece of bamboo, steel or wood to "hold" a big fish. As a matter of fact, few rods are ever broken in actual fishing; very few indeed when handled with a reasonable amount of care.

It is true that it is usually the big fish that gets away, but this is because the big fellow generally puts up a harder fight and the angler in his anxiety to land him takes undue liberties with rod, line, and hook—more often the line. Also one's style of casting has much to do with the losing or hooking of fish. It is more than a mere coincidence that the man who cannot start his bait back quickly loses so many fish. Especially when fishing with artificial baits should the lure be started back before or the very instant it strikes the water. As stated before this can be done by giving the rod a twitch to one side with the left hand as one shifts hands preliminary to reeling in. As the bait is being retrieved the rod-tip should be kept pointing at it, at all times being lowered gradually as the bait nears the boat.

We give this advice with the full realization that many expert casters reel in with the rod-butt resting on their chests and the rod-tip pointing almost straight up in the air. They learned this way in the early days, or got the habit from someone who did, and they find it hard to change. Most of them, if you will press the point, will admit that it is the wrong way.

When the rod-tip is pointing at the bait you are always in a position to strike quickly, which is done by giving a slight jerk upward with the rod to set the hooks. The mouth roofs of most fishes caught by bait casting are bony in structure and the hook always should be driven home. When reeling with the rod-tip pointing up, unless you are very expert with the rod, you are very likely to strike too late; also if you should get a strike near the boat (and sometimes they come right out from under the boat) you are likely to smash the tip of your rod. By all means learn to reel with your rod-tip low and do not let anyone talk you into doing it any other way unless it be for the purpose of keeping the line dry.

After the fish is hooked you should play him or tire

him out before attempting to land him. This is done by making the fish pull against the bend in your rod. Therefore, keep the tip of your rod up while playing a fish so there is always a strain on it. This not only tires the fish but prevents him getting any slack line which would enable him to eject or shake the hook from his mouth. Under no circumstances should the fish be given any slack. The fish should be reeled in whenever he will permit it and he should be given line grudgingly. That is, when the strain on your tackle becomes dangerous, allow the fish to run a way, but always keep your thumb on the spooled line with enough pressure to keep a pronounced bend in the rod.

If the water is very weedy or there are obstructions like logs, pilings, etc., tackle heavy enough to stand "hammer and tongs" fishing should be used and the fish given no opportunity to foul the line. If the water is fairly open the fish can be given his head a little, but remember, the longer the line the better chance the fish has of getting away.

Many kinds of advice are offered to the novice as to what measures to follow when a fish leaps. Generally speaking, the rule is to raise the rod a trifle when he leaps on a long line and to lower it when he falls back into the water to prevent him falling on a taut line and thus tearing the hook from his mouth. If the fish gains any slack in this process it should be taken up again as soon as he strikes the water. When he leaps on a short line the novice usually does nothing as the fish is out and back again so quickly and the natural spring of the rod ordinarily prevents the fish from getting any slack.

When a very heavy fish, like a muskellunge for instance, leaps, the rod is raised as he goes out of the water just enough to keep the spoon on a level with the hook. One can tell when a fish, especially a fish that is fighting deep, is going to leap by the amount of slack the angler is getting, and he can prepare for it, meanwhile taking up the slack as fast as possible with the reel.

When fishing from a boat, much of the success in landing fish depends on the man at the oars. As soon as a big fish is hooked he should move the boat so as to give the angler every possible advantage. Particularly when fishing over a weed-bed should he head the boat toward open water. Very often in playing a fish he will dash straight at the boat and go under, and this requires some fast reeling and quick thinking, The oarsman should raise his oars to prevent the line tangling on them and the angler should pass his rod around the end of the boat and fight the fish from the other side.

Landing fish properly also is an art in itself. When a net is used it should be submerged and the fish led over it instead of trying to scoop the fish into the net. Big fish should be landed with a gaff hook. The hook should be struck into the fish from below, well back toward the tail and the fish should be gaffed, lifted from the water, and swung into the boat with one motion—this requires practice.

The caster should learn to land his own fish as he may do some fishing alone. This is done, after the fish has been played, by holding the rod with the rod hand extended so that it curves over the top of his head and the landing net or gaff hook is manipulated with the other hand. This is best done by kneeling in the bottom of the boat; otherwise one may literally get a taste of "fisherman's luck."

WEATHER AND OTHER THINGS INFLUENCING FISHERMAN'S LUCK

For ages fishermen have pondered over the question of why fish will "bite" well on one day and not on another. Some anglers attribute their success or failure to "luck" and let it go at that, while others believe that the weather exerts considerable influence on the fish. The seasons of the year affect the feeding habits of the fish and we all know that the fish are apparently more hungry, or at least bite better, in the spring and fall than in midsummer.

Coming to the subject of weather, we are of the opinion that the weather three or four days previous to the time we try our luck has as much to do with the results as the conditions prevailing while we are on the water. Generally, the ideal fishing day is what any non-angler would call a "nice day"—when the atmosphere is clear, the weather invigorating, the sun fairly bright, and a slight breeze ruffling the surface of the water. Equally good from the fishing standpoint is the cloudy overcast day, if the weather is not too cool for comfort, when it threatens to rain and doesn't. The few hours just before a warm rain are also proverbially good.

After a very heavy shower or severe thunderstorm the water is usually too roily for good fishing and several days must elapse for things to settle down to normal conditions. Our observations lead us to believe that bass are not afraid of thunder, but at the first flash of lightning they will head for deep water and stay there until the storm has passed.

Much blame for poor fishing is attached to an east or northeast wind, although personally we believe that neither has any particular effect one way or the other, further than that an east wind, if it blows long enough, is bound to bring a rain and a northeaster, usually a cold, blustering storm. Generally, however, the influence of the direction of the wind is grossly exaggerated and the same may be said of the phases of the moon. The velocity of the wind, providing it does not reach the gale stage, is not ordinarily of a great deal of importance either, except as it affects our comfort. A breeze just strong enough to put a riffle on the water is ideal, but if it exceeds this very much it usually means that we must fish in sheltered places such as bays or the lee shore. Fishing the lee shore in a high wind is a common practice and apparently it is productive of fish, too.

Sometimes the fish are in a "biting" mood. Even when their stomachs are apparently filled they will strike a lure either in anger or in the spirit of play. It is generally accepted by anglers that game fish, being night feeders, the ones we catch in the daytime are the few that did not get a "square feed" the night before and this is the logical explanation of the fact that only a very small percentage of the available fish are ever striking at one time. It is well that this is so, otherwise the fish would soon be exterminated.

The best hours for fishing are usually from daybreak until say ten in the morning, or from four in the afternoon until midnight, varying somewhat with the seasons and peculiar local conditions. On cloudy days fish seem to strike well all day, as is often the case with a bright sun in cold weather.

Personally, we believe that early morning fishing on large lakes is seldom worth missing one's breakfast. Our experience is that it is just as well to wait until the sun is up. Local conditions vary, however, and the man who lives near good fishing waters soon learns by observation just what the conditions should be for a good day. The conditions that spell a good day and a big string on one piece of water may have an opposite effect on another.

CHAPTER X

A MIXED STRING

Tournament Casting

TOURNAMENT casting bears about the same relationship to fishing that trap shooting does to hunting. It is practice in a way and besides is a sport in itself. In the city of Chicago alone there are about nine clubs with a total membership of six hundred and the movement is growing throughout the country. Nearly all the clubs in this country are affiliated with the National Association of Scientific Angling Clubs or the National Amateur Casting Association, which is good, inasmuch as it standardizes the work and makes for better co-operation.

It does not require a great deal of paraphernalia nor a large amount of money to start a casting club and it is intensely interesting and does much to interest the community in scientific angling and, incidentally, conservation.

Personally, we are of the opinion that tournament casting is too highly specialized to be of the greatest value, but this no doubt will adjust itself as the tendency is more and more toward practical work.

The rod used in tournament work is ordinarily made for the purpose and usually is of bamboo. Lengths and weights vary, but the following description of two rods from a well-known maker's catalog will give one some idea as to what is considered good:

"Light Single-Piece Rod, for quarter ounce casting, 5¼ feet long, about 4¼ ounces weight, with independent single grasp handle 9 inches long, agate guide next to hand and agate tip."

"Medium Single-Piece Rod, for half ounce casting, 5¼ feet long, about 5½ ounces weight, otherwise same as above."

Many tournament casters make their own rods or have them made on their own specifications. The tournament fly rod is an ideal rod for fishing and it is unfortunate that the same can not be said of the tournament bait casting rod.

An ordinary fishing reel is too sluggish for tournament work and special reels are made for this purpose. They are usually jeweled and unless free spool equipped with very small handles to minimize air resistance. A high grade tournament reel costs from twenty-five dollars up.

The line used in tournament casting is oo or ooo white silk, machine twist. Ordinarily this is used with a leader of heavy silk such as A silk thread or the regular braided tournament line. Braided tournament lines test from five to ten pounds and are often used although they are not as popular as formerly. ·

The rules governing tournament casting as specified by the National Association of Scientific Angling Clubs are, briefly, as follows:

The target is a huge spider-web affair 12 feet 6 inches in diameter. It consists of six concentric rings placed twelve inches apart with an inner ring thirty inches in diameter, in the center of which is a bulls-eye, not over six inches in diameter. This target should be so constructed that all but the bulls-eye will be submerged just below the surface. The target is arranged so that it can be moved by a cable to the various casting distances.

One-half ounce accuracy bait casting is done at 60, 70, 80, 90, and 100 feet. Each contestant casts once at each distance consecutively and then reverses the order, making ten casts in all. If the weight falls in the thirty-inch circle the cast is perfect and for each foot or fraction of a foot away from the thirty-inch center a demerit of one is made. The sum total of such demerits divided by the number of casts is the demerit per cent. The demerit per cent deducted from 100 constitutes the percentage. The quarter ounce accuracy is scored the same except that the official quarter ounce weight is used instead of the half ounce and the distances are 60, 65, 70, 75, and 80 feet.

Distance casting is done on a V-shaped court on the lawn and the length of cast is computed from casting point to where weight falls inside of court. The sum total of five casts in feet divided by the number of casts made shall be the average and the contestant's score.   Both half and quarter ounce weights are used in distance casting.

In addition to these events many clubs are taking up what one might call "practical" work. At least one Chicago club has a "Pork Chunk Casting Contest." Regular fishing lines are used and the chunk is cast over the same distances as in quarter ounce casting and the scoring for accuracy is done in the usual manner.   For jumping or skipping the chunk for a distance exceeding one foot when starting to retrieve a demerit of one is made and the same if chunk is allowed to remain under water for a distance of more than three feet after starting to retrieve as well as when the chunk is permitted to sink below the surface during the retrieve.   The sum total of such demerits on style divided by the number of casts constitutes the demerit per cent.   The demerit per cent from 100 per cent constitutes the combined percentage of style and accuracy.

Other events along similar lines, such as casting plugs both from the platform and when seated in a boat, casting spinners and flies, do a great deal in attracting fishermen, many of them expert, who can see no merit in tournament casting and speak of tournament casters as "park fishermen" and "tin can artists." The young caster can make no mistake in joining a casting club, or organizing one if there are none in the vicinity, as it will help make him a better caster and will bring him in contact with many expert anglers to say nothing of the value of concerted action along conservation lines.

PRACTICAL FISH CONSERVATION

When the white man first settled in what is now the United States, the lakes and streams teemed with game fishes of all kinds. For example, up until 1840 trout were plentiful in the Chagrin River, a few miles east of Cleveland, Ohio, and other near-by streams, while to-day there is only one trout stream in the whole state of Ohio, and that an artificially stocked one, the property of a fishing club. In the Elkhorn and other streams of Kentucky, muskellunge and immense pike-perch were common, but these streams know them no more. In practically every lake and stream in the Great Lakes region, black bass were plentiful; now there are hundreds of waters where the black bass is either unknown or very rare unless artificially stocked. What is the reason?

Several causes. Civilization and the consequent, although unnecessary, pollution of water is one; the hoggishness of man is another.

Most fishermen, commercial as well as sporting, look upon our State and Fish Commissions,, as a police force to enforce more or less obnoxious laws that are, according to their viewpoint, designed solely to interfere with fishing. As a matter of fact, the enforcement of laws is only incidental; the real purpose of a State commission is to conserve for both present and future generations, the fish and game resources of the state. Due to the shortsightedness of the people most interested, game and fish laws and their enforcement are necessary. In the language of one of the comic newspaper characters: "Them is harsh words," but the situation, to one who has studied the facts, demands harshness.

In many ways the fish laws of most states are quite uniform, modified only to suit local conditions. For example, in most northern states the open season for bass begins at or near the average end of the spawning season. Only two states in the Middle West, Illinois and Indiana, have no closed season; the latter state, however, fences off the spawning beds and permits no fishing on them up to July 1st.

The decrease of game fishes would be a great deal more noticeable if it were not for the breeding and stocking operations carried on by most states. Certain fishes, such as trout, salmon, perch, pike-perch, pickerel, and muskellunge are hatched artificially by stripping the eggs from the female and fertilizing them with milt stripped from the male. The eggs are then placed in jars or trays and water of a certain temperature kept flowing over them. Incubation takes place, depending on the species and the water temperature, in from 25 to 90 days.

The equipment for hatching fish need not be elaborate, the work is not difficult nor complicated, and many individuals and clubs are taking up the artificial hatching of fish with very good results. As many as 95 per cent of the eggs from a muskellunge have been hatched artificially, while in a state of nature a tenth of that would probably be a big hatch.

With the black bass we experience something else, because it is not practicable to hatch them artificially. The female suffers a severe nervous shock when handled, which prevents easy stripping of spawn, and the adhesive character of the eggs makes them difficult, almost impossible, to fertilize. In spite of these limitations, however, the propagation of black bass is now being done on a large scale. In Illinois, for example, the state hatchery at Spring Grove turns out upward of a million bass fry annually, and their capacity is steadily being increased.

The propagation of the black bass is being done by permitting the fish to mate and spawn naturally under favorable conditions, and the good results obtained are due to the care the young receive after they are hatched.

A female bass will yield as much as 25 per cent of her weight in eggs. In the natural state but a small proportion of these ever become mature fish, due to the numerous enemies the young bass have to contend with. Not only do perch, minnows, and other fishes prey on them, but the little rascals are terrible cannibals. The small mouth bass hardly reaches the advanced fry stage, when he commences to prey on his brothers, and the large mouth is a cannibal from the yearling stage on.

Parenthetically, while this cannibalism in the bass

family is a source of annoyance and worry to the fish culturist, it is in our opinion not without its advantages. The fact that the black bass is so self-reliant, so active, such a hard fighter is due in great part, to the bitter struggle for survival that he encounters from the time he breaks through the egg.

The work of hatching and caring for bass as carried on in a modern bass plant is simple but interesting. Artificial nests, simply boxes of gravel, are made, or the male fish is permitted to construct his own nest in favorable positions, then comes the courtship and the fertilizing of the eggs as described elsewhere in this book. When the eggs are hatched, the nest is surrounded by a "crib" or screen and in a few days the entire hatch is removed to the fry ponds especially made to rear young fish.

The Illinois hatchery, which is the largest in the country, consists of a main breeding pond of 13 acres, and a number of rearing ponds of an acre each. These are arranged so that they receive a continual supply of fresh water and the water in each pond can be lowered for seining out the fry or, if necessary, can be drained entirely.

While a plant of this kind is needed by the state of Illinois, with its hundreds of lakes and streams, hatcheries are also doing good work locally. An example worthy of special mention is the Bass Lake Hatchery at Bass Lake, Ind. This is run on the co-operative plan. The state, we believe, constructed the ponds and put them under the care of the local deputy warden. The Bass Lake Improvement Association helps defray the expenses. This association is made up of the local merchants, hotel keepers, and cottagers, and all contribute to its support.

Their plant is very modest, consisting of only four ponds each about one hundred feet square, and the water is obtained by tapping a near-by spring. With this little equipment they raise and put into the lake thousands of bass every year and in a few years they no doubt will have one of the best bass fishing lakes in the Middle West. The Association is fortunate in having such a conscientious and efficient warden and propagator as Mr. Peter Lavery; also in the fact that the lake is exceptionally well stocked with minnows so that the breeding bass are fed on them the year round.

Improvement associations are not uncommon around resort waters, but few of them accomplish much. The Bass Lake Association is an example that others could follow to very good advantage.

The organization of casting clubs to interest the people in scientific angling, then the improvement association, then the local hatchery and the enforcement of reasonable laws, especially as regards pollution—all these are needed to bring the native game fishes back to our waters and before many years have passed this method of conservation, we believe, will be common throughout the settled portions of the United States.

Starting a bass breeding plant is surprisingly simple.

Established ponds can be utilized or they can be secured by excavating or by damming a stream or, better still, by diverting a stream and building dikes to hold the water. Care should be taken to avoid having the pond directly in the course of a stream or having it so situated that surface water can drain in after a heavy rain.

The pond need not be deep—say two feet at the edges for a breeding shelf and not less than six feet deep in the center so as to prevent asphyxiation during a heavy freeze. A plant consisting of two ponds, a breeding and wintering pond and a rearing pond, is better than a single body of water.

The best procedure is to first plant water vegetation such as pond weed, cress, duckweed, pickerel grass, spatterdock, and chara moss. These can be taken from near-by waters, pulled up roots and all and thrown into the pond fastened to stones to anchor them until they are established. These plants furnish food in the form of cyclops, water lice, and other minute crustacea and shelter for both the rearing and food fish. Food fish for the breeders can be shiners, chubs, or other minnows, say about one hundred pairs to start with. Other food such as crawfish and frogs should also be provided if possible.

Advanced fry of the breeder fish may be planted in the pond the first summer, fingerlings in the fall and mature fish the following spring. About twenty-five or thirty pairs of adult fish, two thousand advanced fry or from four to six thousand fry is about the right number to start with for an acre pond. Local conditions have much to do with how this work is carried on, but both the State and Federal governments have experts who will give free advice on these points; the State also will supply the breeders or fry free of charge. It is very simple. Results? Here is one example taken from an Indiana State Report:

In May Carl H. Thompson, of Huntington County, Ind., placed fourteen pairs of small mouth bass in a pond measuring 60 x 120 feet, and from 4 to 6 feet deep. Fifteen months later he drained the pond and took out ten hundred and seventeen bass averaging a pound in weight.

THE RULES OF THE GAME

The ethics of bait casting are about the same as those of any other style of fishing. Reasonably light tackle, moderation in the size of one's string, the returning of small fish to the water, and doing one's share of the work just about sums it up.

Light tackle can be overdone, although it must be said that the opposite extreme is more common. The tackle should be in accordance with the style of fishing and the prevailing conditions. It is not sportsmanship to fish for heavy fish with tackle so light that there is much likelihood of your fish breaking away with a hook or bait fast in its jaw.

As to the size of the string, this must be determined by circumstances. It is not a good plan to take more fish than you can use, not only from the standpoint of sportsmanship but from the more selfish one of spoiling one's future fishing.   Most states have a legal limit of ten, twelve, or fifteen fish per day and these limits are very generous.

The minimum legal size for bass in most states is ten inches, but, except in case of small mouth bass in streams, where they are inclined to run small, it is not wisdom to keep fish of this size.   A ten-inch bass weighs scarcely a pound and under favorable conditions he will almost double that weight in a year—always give the fish the benefit of the doubt.

Fish to be returned to the water should be handled as little as possible and then only with wet hands. Dry hands rub off the protecting slime and this renders the fish susceptible to fungus diseases, especially if the water is warm.   Holding a bass by the lower jaw with the thumb in the mouth prevents his wriggling and permits easy removal of the hook.

The labor incident to fishing should be equally distributed.   When two men fish from a boat, both can cast when drifting with the wind or flow and each should do his share of rowing back.   In case there is a high wind "to buck" using two pairs of oars will probably be the most satisfactory.   In stream fishing from a boat one should be at the oars or handle the paddle while the other is fishing.   When working three in a boat one should be at the oars while the other two fish.

Fishing two men to a boat is probably the most satisfactory unless the third man is a hired oarsman. When one hooks a fish the other should stop fishing, take the oars, and obey orders, rowing where directed and assisting as much as possible in the landing of the prize. Not only that, but he should unhook the fish and string it while his partner is getting his line and lure ready for another cast. If a fish is not played properly and is lost, don't criticize or offer suggestions unless they are asked for. In other words, each man of the party should exert himself to be as useful and as companionable as possible.

Writing on the ethics of fishing is a hard job because it may sound like preaching, but we offer these few suggestions for the benefit of the beginner and to possibly save him some disagreeable experiences. The youngster should ever bear in mind that to have the reputation of being a true sportsman is better far than to be known as merely a "crack" fisherman.

MISCELLANEOUS EQUIPMENT

Although the outfit of the modern bait caster may be very simple, as one's interest develops he finds that there are many little things outside of the tackle line that add to his success or comfort. We append a few remarks on this subject that may be of help.

BOATS

The best boat for casting is flat bottomed. While most casting should be done sitting down it is sometimes desirable to make a cast or two while standing. This is risky in a round bottom or "clinker" boat and decidedly dangerous in a canoe. Besides the caster is often out in rough weather and a seaworthy craft is more comfortable to fish from.

If the caster buys a boat or has one made to order it is a good plan to have it heavy enough in the stern to take an outboard motor.

OUTBOARD MOTORS

The outboard or rowboat motor is a blessing to the bait caster because of the amount of water one covers in a day's fishing due to the roaming habits of the bass, his principal quarry. These motors weight in the neighborhood of fifty pounds, and are therefore easily transported. As now made they are very dependable.

CUSHIONS

Sitting all day on the "soft side of a board seat" becomes uncomfortable, so a cushion is of decided value. A simple one can be a bag made of drill or canvas which is carried empty and filled with hay or grass when the fishing grounds are reached. More comfortable is the pneumatic rubber ring which can be carried flat and is easily inflated when wanted. Personally, we use the small (twelve-inch) size but this would hardly do for those made along the lines of "Big Built Aft." For one's boat at the permanent camp, I recommend the Kapoc cushion, which in case of

emergency will act as a life preserver, as one will
float a full-grown man.

CLOTHING

Almost any old thing in the clothing line will do for
fishing, but suitable garments add to one's comfort and
health. For fishing early and late in the season, when
the mornings and evenings are a bit chilly, woolen un-
derwear and woolen socks should be worn. Waterproof moccasins of light weight or light cruisers are
good footwear for this time of the year, but in midsummer shoes of ordinary leather will be more comfortable, as "waterproof" leather of any kind is warm.

For an all-around shirt, nothing equals the olive drab
army shirt with two patch pockets—one for the watch
and the other for the pipe and "baccy" or compass.
For trousers, we prefer the Duxbak or heavy khaki riding trousers except in hot weather when light weight
drill is preferable. Many out-door men wear the
regular army campaign hat but our choice is an un-
lined khaki cap with cape or earlaps to keep out the
rain or to protect the neck from sun, flies, and mosquitoes. For a jacket a waterproof hunting coat is
satisfactory, although the light weight rubber fishing
shirts that fold and go into the tackle box are hard to
beat for convenience.

For wading the regular trout stream waders that
come to the waist should have first choice. Woolen
socks should be worn both inside and outside of these—

the outside ones to protect the rubber from chafing.

The regulation wading shoes are expensive but good; the adjustable sandals are also satisfactory. Tennis slippers may be worn over waders when wading shoes are not to be had or when the bottom is not too rocky. For shallow streams hip boots are satisfactory—don't forget a few patches for emergencies. For casting in cold weather rubber lined gloves with the right thumb cut off will be found a comfort.

Cook Kits

Every caster should own one of the simple little compact cook kits now on the market. It makes you independent of hotels and it must be remembered that the best fishing is usually had at breakfast and supper times. Another friend to the fisherman is the bottle that keeps liquids cold or hot for a considerable period. The surface water of most fishing lakes and streams is not fit to drink and one of these bottles "loaded" in advance with spring water, cold tea, or some other refreshment is truly a blessing on a hot day. Also hot coffee or tea is not "hard to take" in cool weather.

The Last Cast

Abler pens than ours have sung the praises of angling, of the delights of a day afloat or of wading the stream, and many have spoken of the healthfulness, of the fresh air and sunshine. Few, however, have said much of the relaxation and restfulness scientific angling brings to tired workers. Non-anglers may wonder how one can gain rest by working at the oars, wading a stream, or wielding a rod for hours at a time as patient fishermen must and do. Perhaps the following statement made by a well-known psychologist will throw some light on this subject:

"A study of adult sports shows that those sports which afford the most complete relaxation and recreation are forms racially old and familiar and hence easy and restful. They involve not the higher and newer brain tracts but the older and more basal ones. Hunting, fishing, camping, boating, and all the many forms of outing are familiar illustrations."*

The camaraderie, the sunshine, the fresh air and the work of bait casting make up one way to cheat Father Time and to keep our youth and enthusiasm without which Life, indeed, would be a humdrum affair and—well, never mind the philosophizing. Here's luck and may your days be long on the water and may your creels be decently heavy—and decently light.

THE END

---

*G. T. W. Patrick in "Interstate Medical Journal."

OUTING

HANDBOOKS
The textbooks for out-door work and play

Each book deals with a separate subject and deals with it thoroughly. If you want to know anything about Airedales an OUTING HANDBOOK gives you all you want. If it's Apple Growing, another OUTING HANDBOOK meets your need. The Fisherman, the Camper, the Poultry-raiser, the Automobilist, the Horseman, all varieties of out-door enthusiasts, will find separate volumes for their separate interests. There is no waste space.

The series is based on the plan of one subject to a book and each book complete. The authors are experts. Each book has been specially prepared for this series and all are published in uniform style, flexible cloth binding.

Two hundred titles are projected. The series covers all phases of outdoor life, from bee-keeping to big-game shooting. Among the books now ready or in preparation are those described on the following pages.

If you wish for any information on any outdoor subject not treated in one of the following books write Outing Publishing Co., 141-145 West 36th St., New York.

PRICE EIGHTY CENTS PER VOL. NET,
POSTAGE 5c. EXTRA
THE NUMBERS MAKE ORDERING EASY.

1. **EXERCISE AND HEALTH, by Dr. Woods Hutchinson.** Dr. Hutchinson takes the common-sense view that the greatest problem in exercise for most of us is to get enough of the right kind. The greatest error in exercise is not to take enough, and the greatest danger in athletics is in giving them up. He writes in a direct matter-of-fact manner with an avoidance of medical terms, and a strong emphasis on the rational, all-around manner of living that is best calculated to bring a man to a ripe old age with little illness or consciousness of bodily weakness.

17

2.   CAMP COOKERY, by Horace Kephart.

"The less a man carries in his pack the more he must carry in his head," says Mr. Kephart. This book tells what a man should carry in both pack and head. Every step is traced—the selection of provisions and utensils, with the kind and quantity of each, the preparation of game, the building of fires, the cooking of every conceivable kind of food that the camp outfit or woods, fields or streams may provide—even to the making of desserts. Every recipe is the result of hard practice and long experience.

3.   BACKWOODS   SURGERY   AND MEDICINE, by Charles S. Moody, M. D.   A

handy book for the prudent lover of the woods who doesn't expect to be ill but believes in being on the safe side. Common-sense methods for the treatment of the ordinary wounds and accidents are described— setting a broken limb, reducing a dislocation, caring for burns, cuts, etc. Practical remedies for camp diseases are recommended, as well as the ordinary indications of the most probable ailments. Includes a list of the necessary medical and surgical supplies.

4.   APPLE GROWING, by M. C. Burritt.

The various problems confronting the apple grower, from the preparation of the soil and the planting of the trees to the marketing of the fruit, are discussed in detail by the author.

5.   THE AIREDALE, by Williams Haynes.

The book opens with a short chapter on the origin and development of the Airedale, as a distinctive breed. The author then takes up the problems of type as bearing on the selection of the dog, breeding, training and use. The book is designed for the non-professional dog fancier, who wishes common sense advice which does not involve elaborate preparations or expenditure. Chapters are included on the care of the dog in the kennel and simple remedies for ordinary diseases.

6. THE AUTOMOBILE — Its Selection, Care and Use, by Robert Sloss. This is a plain, practical discussion of the things that every man needs to know if he is to buy the right car and get the most out of it. The various details of operation and care are given in simple, intelligent terms. From it the car owner can easily learn the mechanism of his motor and the art of locating motor trouble, as well as how to use his car for the greatest pleasure.

7. FISHING KITS AND EQUIPMENT, by Samuel G. Camp. A complete guide to the angler buying a new outfit. Every detail of the fishing kit of the freshwater angler is described, from rodtip to creel, and clothing. Special emphasis is laid on outfitting for fly fishing, but full instruction is also given to the man who wants to catch pickerel, pike, muskellunge, lake-trout, bass and other freshwater game fishes. The approved method of selecting and testing the various rods, lines, leaders, etc., is described.

8. THE FINE ART OF FISHING, by Samuel G. Camp. Combine the pleasure of catching fish with the gratification of following the sport in the most approved manner. The suggestions offered are helpful to beginner and expert anglers. The range of fish and fishing conditions covered is wide and includes such subjects as "Casting Fine and Far Off," "Strip-Casting for Bass," "Fishing for Mountain Trout" and "Autumn Fishing for Lake Trout." The book is pervaded with a spirit of love for the streamside and the out-doors generally which the genuine angler will appreciate. A companion book to "Fishing Kits and Equipment."

9. THE HORSE — Its Breeding, Care and Use, by David Buffum. Mr. Buffum takes up the common, every-day problems of the ordinary horse-users, such as feeding, shoeing, simple home remedies, breaking and the cure for various equine vices. An important chapter is that tracing the influx of Arabian blood into the English and American horses and its value and limitations. A distinctly sensible book for the sensible man who wishes to know how he can improve his horses and his horsemanship at the same time.

19

10. THE MOTOR BOAT—Its Selection, Care and Use, by H. W. Slauson. The intending purchaser is advised as to the type of motor boat best suited to his particular needs and how to keep it in running condition after purchased.

11. OUTDOOR SIGNALLING, by Elbert Wells. Mr. Wells has perfected a method of signalling by means of wigwag, light, smoke, or whistle which is as simple as it is effective. The fundamental principle can be learned in ten minutes and its application is far easier than that of any other code now in use.

12. TRACKS AND TRACKING, by Josef Brunner. After twenty years of patient study and practical experience, Mr. Brunner can, from his intimate knowledge, speak with authority on this subject. "Tracks and Tracking" shows how to follow intelligently even the most intricate animal or bird tracks; how to interpret tracks of wild game and decipher the many tell-tale signs of the chase that would otherwise pass unnoticed; to tell from the footprints the name, sex, speed, direction, whether and how wounded, and many other things about wild animals and birds.

13. WING AND TRAP-SHOOTING, by Charles Askins. Contains a full discussion of the various methods, such as snap-shooting, swing and half-swing, discusses the flight of birds with reference to the gunner's problem of lead and range and makes special application of the various points to the different birds commonly shot in this country. A chapter is included on trap shooting and the book closes with a forceful and common-sense presentation of the etiquette of the field.

14. PROFITABLE BREEDS OF POULTRY, by Arthur S. Wheeler. Mr. Wheeler discusses from personal experience the best-known general purpose breeds. Advice is given from the standpoint of the man who desires results in eggs and stock rather than in specimens for exhibition. In addition to a careful analysis of stock—good and bad—and some conclusions regarding housing and management, the author writes in detail regarding Plymouth Rocks, Wyandottes, Orpingtons, Rhode Island Reds, etc.

15. RIFLES AND RIFLE SHOOTING,

by Charles Askins. A practical manual describing various makes and mechanisms, in addition to discussing in detail the range and limitations in the use of the rifle. Treats on the every style and make of rifle as well as their use. Every type of rifle is discussed so that the book is complete in every detail.

16. SPORTING FIREARMS, by Horace

Kephart. This book is the result of painstaking tests and experiments. Practically nothing is taken for granted. Part I deals with the rifle, and Part II with the shotgun. The man seeking guidance in the selection and use of small firearms, as well as the advanced student of the subject, will receive an unusual amount of assistance from this work.

17. THE YACHTSMAN'S HANDBOOK,

by Herbert L. Stone. The author and compiler of this work is the editor of "Yachting." He treats in simple language of the many problems confronting the amateur sailor and motor boatman. Handling ground tackle, handling lines, taking soundings, the use of the lead line, care and use of sails, yachting etiquette, are all given careful attention. Some light is thrown upon the operation of the gasoline motor, and suggestions are made for the avoidance of engine troubles.

18. SCOTTISH AND IRISH TERRIERS,

by Williams Haynes. This is a companion book to "The Airedale," and deals with the history and development of both breeds. For the owner of the dog, valuable information is given as to the use of the terriers, their treatment in health, their treatment when sick, the principles of dog breeding, and dog shows and rules.

19. NAVIGATION FOR THE AMA-

TEUR, by Capt. E. T. Morton. A short treatise on the simpler methods of finding position at sea by the observation of the sun's altitude and the use of the sextant and chronometer. It is arranged especially for yachtsmen and amateurs who wish to know the simpler formulæ for the necessary navigation involved in taking a boat anywhere off shore. Illustrated.

20. OUTDOOR PHOTOGRAPHY, by Julian A. Dimock.

A solution of all the problems in camera work out-of-doors. The various subjects dealt with are: The Camera—Lens and Plates—Light and Exposure—Development—Prints and Printing, etc.

21. PACKING AND PORTAGING, by Dillon Wallace.

Mr. Wallace has brought together in one volume all the valuable information on the different ways of making and carrying the different kinds of packs. The ground covered ranges from man-packing to horse-packing, from the use of the tump line to throwing the diamond hitch.

22. THE BULL TERRIER, by Williams Haynes.

This is a companion book to "The Airedale" and "Scottish and Irish Terriers" by the same author. Its greatest usefulness is as a guide to the dog owner who wishes to be his own kennel manager. A full account of the development of the breed is given with a description of best types and standards. Recommendations for the care of the dog in health or sickness are included.

23. THE FOX TERRIER, by Williams Haynes.

As in his other books on the terrier, Mr. Haynes takes up the origin and history of the breed, its types and standards, and the more exclusive representatives down to the present time. Training the Fox Terrier—His Care and Kenneling in Sickness and Health—and the Various Uses to Which He Can Be Put—are among the phases handled.

24. SUBURBAN GARDENS, by Grace Tabor.

Illustrated with diagrams. The author regards the house and grounds as a complete unit and shows how the best results may be obtained by carrying the reader in detail through the various phases of designing the garden, with the levels and contours necessary, laying out the walks and paths, planning and placing the arbors, summer houses, seats, etc., and selecting and placing trees, shrubs, vines and flowers. Ideal plans for plots of various sizes are appended, as well as suggestions for correcting mistakes that have been made through "starting wrong."

25. FISHING WITH FLOATING FLIES,

by Samuel G. Camp. This is an art that is comparatively new in this country although English anglers have used the dry fly for generations. Mr. Camp has given the matter special study and is one of the few American anglers who really understands the matter from the selection of the outfit to the landing of the fish.

26. THE GASOLINE MOTOR, by Harold

Whiting Slauson. Deals with the practical problems of motor operation. The standpoint is that of the man who wishes to know how and why gasoline generates power and something about the various types. Describes in detail the different parts of motors and the faults to which they are liable. Also gives full directions as to repair and upkeep.

27. ICE BOATING, by H. L. Stone. Illus-

trated with diagrams. Here have been brought together all the available information on the organization and history of ice-boating, the building of the various types of ice yachts, from the small 15 footer to the 600-foot racer, together with detailed plans and specifications. Full information is also given to meet the needs of those who wish to be able to build and sail their own boats but are handicapped by the lack of proper knowledge as to just the points described in this volume.

28. MODERN GOLF, by Harold H. Hil-

ton. Mr. Hilton is the only man who has ever held the amateur championship of Great Britain and the United States in the same year. This book gives the reader sound advice, not so much on the mere swinging of the clubs as in the actual playing of the game, with all the factors that enter into it. He discusses the use of wooden clubs, the choice of clubs, the art of approaching, and kindred subjects.

29. INTENSIVE FARMING, by L. C.

Corbett. A discussion of the meaning, method and value of intensive methods in agriculture. This book is designed for the convenience of practical farmers who find themselves under the necessity of making a living out of high-priced land.

30. PRACTICAL DOG BREEDING, by
Williams Haynes. This is a companion volume to PRACTICAL DOG KEEPING, described below. It goes at length into the fundamental questions of breeding, such as selection of types on both sides, the perpetuation of desirable, and the elimination of undesirable qualities, the value of prepotency in building up a desired breed, etc.

31. PRACTICAL DOG KEEPING, by
Williams Haynes. Mr. Haynes is well known to the readers of the OUTING HANDBOOKS as the author of books on the terriers. His new book is somewhat more ambitious in that it carries him into the general field of selection of breeds, the buying and selling of dogs, the care of dogs in kennels, handling in bench shows and field trials, and at considerable length into such subjects as food and feeding, exercise and grooming, disease, etc.

32. THE VEGETABLE GARDEN, by R.
L. Watts. This book is designed for the small grower with a limited plot of ground. The reader is told what types of vegetables to select, the manner of planting and cultivation, and the returns that may be expected.

33. AMATEUR RODMAKING, by Perry
D. Frazer. Illustrated. A practical manual for all those who want to make their own rod and fittings. It contains a review of fishing rod history, a discussion of materials, a list of the tools needed, description of the method to be followed in making all kinds of rods, including fly-casting, bait-fishing, salmon, etc., with full instructions for winding, varnishing, etc.

34. PISTOL AND REVOLVER SHOOT-
ING, by A. L. A. Himmelwright. A new and revised edition of a work that has already achieved prominence as an accepted authority on the use of the hand gun. Full instructions are given in the use of both revolver and target pistol, including shooting position, grip, position of arm, etc. The book is thoroughly illustrated with diagrams and photographs and includes the rules of the United States Revolver Association and a list of the records made both here and abroad.

35. PIGEON RAISING, by Alice Mac-
Leod. This is a book for both fancier and market breeder. Full descriptions are given of the construction of houses, the care of the birds, preparation for market, and shipment, of the various breeds with their markings and characteristics.

36. FISHING TACKLE, by Perry D.
Frazer. Illustrated. It tells all the fisherman needs to know about making and overhauling his tackle during the closed season and gives full instructions for tournament casting and fly-casting.

37. AUTOMOBILE OPERATION, by A.
L. Brennan, Jr. Illustrated. Tells the plain truth about the little things that every motorist wants to know about his own car. Do you want to cure ignition troubles? Overhaul and adjust your carbureter? Keep your transmission in order? Get the maximum wear out of your tires? Do any other of the hundred and one things that are necessary for the greatest use and enjoyment of your car? Then you will find this book useful.

38. THE FOX HOUND, by Roger D. Wil-
liams. Author of "Horse and Hound." Illustrated. The author is the foremost authority on fox hunting and foxhounds in America. For years he has kept the foxhound studbook, and is the final source of information on all disputed points relating to this breed. His book discusses types, methods of training, kenneling, diseases and all the other practical points relating to the use and care of the hound, etc.

39. SALT WATER GAME FISHING, by
Charles F. Holder. Mr. Holder covers the whole field of his subject devoting a chapter each to such fish as the tuna, the tarpon, amberjack, the sail fish, the yellow-tail, the king fish, the barracuda, the sea bass and the small game fishes of Florida, Porto Rico, the Pacific Coast, Hawaii, and the Philippines. The habits and habitats of the fish are described, together with the methods and tackle for taking them. Illustrated.

25

40. WINTER CAMPING, by Warwick S.

Carpenter. A book that meets the increasing interest in outdoor life in the cold weather. Mr. Carpenter discusses such subjects as shelter equipment, clothing, food, snowshoeing, skiing, and winter hunting, wild life in winter woods, care of frost bite, etc. Illustrated.

41. *WOODCRAFT FOR WOMEN, by

Mrs. Kathrene Gedney Pinkerton. The author has spent several years in the Canadian woods and is thoroughly familiar with the subject from both the masculine and feminine point of view. She gives sound tips on clothing, camping outfit, food supplies, and methods, by which the woman may adjust herself to the outdoor environment.

42. *SMALL BOAT BUILDING, by H.

W. Patterson. Illustrated with diagrams and plans. A working manual for the man who wants to be his own designer and builder. Detail descriptions and drawings are given showing the various stages in the building, and chapters are included on proper materials and details.

43. READING THE WEATHER, by T.

Morris Longstreth. The author gives in detail the various recognized signs for different kinds of weather based primarily on the material worked out by the Government Weather Bureau, gives rules by which the character and duration of storms may be estimated, and gives instructions for sensible use of the barometer. He also gives useful information as to various weather averages for different parts of the country, at different times of the year, and furnishes sound advice for the camper, sportsman, and others who wish to know what they may expect in the weather line.

44. BOXING, by D. C. Hutchison. Practi-

cal instruction for men who wish to learn the first steps in the manly art. Mr. Hutchison writes from long personal experience as an amateur boxer and as a trainer of other amateurs. His instructions are accompanied with full diagrams showing the approved blows and guards. He also gives full directions for training for condition without danger of going stale from overtraining. It is essentially a book for the amateur.

45. TENNIS TACTICS, by Raymond D. Little.

Out of his store of experience as a successful tennis player, Mr. Little has written this practical guide for those who wish to know how real tennis is played. He tells the reader when and how to take the net, discusses the relative merits of the back-court and volleying game and how their proper balance may be achieved; analyzes and appraises the twist service, shows the fundamental necessities of successful doubles play.

46. HOW TO PLAY TENNIS, by James Burns.

This book gives simple, direct instruction from the professional standpoint on the fundamentals of the game. It tells the reader how to hold his racket, how to swing it for the various strokes, how to stand and how to cover the court. These points are illustrated with photographs and diagrams. The author also illustrates the course of the ball in the progress of play and points out the positions of greatest safety and greatest danger.

47. TAXIDERMY, by Leon L. Pray.

Illustrated with diagrams. Being a practical taxidermist, the author at once goes into the question of selection of tools and materials for the various stages of skinning, stuffing and mounting. The subjects whose handling is described are, for the most part, the every-day ones, such as ordinary birds, small mammals, etc., although adequate instructions are included for mounting big game specimens, as well as the preliminary care of skins in hot climates. Full diagrams accompany the text.

48. THE CANOE—ITS SELECTION, CARE AND USE, by Robert E. Pinkerton.

Illustrated with photographs. With proper use the canoe is one of the safest crafts that floats. Mr. Pinkerton tells how that state of safety may be obtained. He gives full instructions for the selection of the right canoe for each particular purpose or set of conditions. Then he tells how it should be used in order to secure the maximum of safety, comfort and usefulness. His own lesson was learned among the Indians of Canada, where paddling is a high art, and the use of the canoe almost as much a matter of course as the wearing of moccasins.

49. HORSE PACKING, by Charles J.
Post. Illustrated with diagrams. This is a complete
description of the hitches, knots, and apparatus used in
making and carrying loads of various kinds on horse-
back. Its basis is the methods followed in the West
and in the American Army. The diagrams are full and
detailed, giving the various hitches and knots at each
of the important stages so that even the novice can
follow and use them. It is the only book ever published on this subject of which this could be said. Full
description is given of the ideal pack animal, as well as
a catalogue of the diseases and injuries to which such
animals are subject.

50. *LEARNING TO SWIM, by L. de B.
Handley. Illustrated. Constructed especially for the
beginner who has no knowledge of the first steps. Ex-
plains the formation of the strokes, how to acquire confidence in the water and gives full details as to the various methods, including those used by experts and rac-
ing swimmers.

51. *SMALL BOAT NAVIGATION, by
Lieut. Com. F. W. Sterling, U. S. N. Retired.
Illustrated with diagrams. A complete description of
the instruments and methods necessary in navigating
small boats in pilot waters, on soundings, and off shore.
Describes the taking of sights for position, the running
of courses, taking soundings, using the chart, plotting
compass courses, etc. Several chapters are given over
to the seamanship side of navigation, explaining the
handling of small boats under various conditions.

52. *TOURING AFOOT, by Dr. C. P.
Fordyce. Illustrated. This book is designed to
meet the growing interest in walking trips and covers
the whole field of outfit and method for trips of varying
length. Various standard camping devices are described and outfits are prescribed for all conditions.
It is based on the assumption that the reader will want
to carry on his own back everything that he requires
for the trip.

53. THE MARINE MOTOR, by Lieut. Com. F. W. Sterling, U. S. N. (Ret.). Illustrated with diagrams. This book is the product of a wide experience on the engineering staff of the United States Navy. It gives careful descriptions of the various parts of the marine motor, their relation to the whole and their method of operation; it also describes the commoner troubles and suggests remedies. The principal types of engines are described in detail with diagrams. The object is primarily to give the novice a good working knowledge of his engine, its operation and care.

54. *THE BEGINNER'S BEE BOOK, by Frank C. Pellett. Illustrated. This book is designed primarily for the small scale bee farmer. It discusses the different varieties of bees and their adaptability to different conditions, the construction of hives, care and feeding at various times of the year, handling of bees, and the types of locations and feed most suitable for bee culture.

55. *THE POINTER, by Williams Haynes. Contains chapters on the history and development of the breed, selection of dog, breeding, kenneling, and training. Also contains information on common sense remedies for ordinary diseases.

56. *THE SETTER, by Williams Haynes. The author takes up the origin and history of the breed, its development, breeding, kenneling, and training. He also discusses the various diseases to which they are subject and treatment therefor.

57. *PRACTICAL BAIT CASTING, by Larry St. John. Illustrated. This book deals with tackle and methods used in catching black bass. It is based upon a wide and varied experience in the middle West, where more bass fishing is done than in any other part of the country.

WS - #0197 - 080724 - C0 - 229/152/11 - PB - 9780243087976 - Gloss Lamination